UPHILL STEPS IN INDIA

UPHILL STEPS IN INDIA

M. L. CHRISTLIED

GYAN

Published by

Gyan Publishing House
5, Ansari Road
Daryaganj, New Delhi-110002
Phone: 011-47034999, 9811692060
E-mail: books@gyanbooks.com

Distribution Network
gyanbooks.com
India, USA, Canada, UK, Australia

ISBN: 978-93-7097-253-7 (PB)

First Published, 1931

2nd Impression 2025

Printed at: Gyan Press, Delhi.

UPHILL STEPS IN INDIA INDIA
Arthur M. L. CHRISTLIED

UPHILL STEPS IN INDIA

UPHILL STEPS IN INDIA

BY

M. L. CHRISTLIEB

1931

TO

ALL MEN AND WOMEN

OF WHATEVER RACE,

WHO LOVE INDIA, AND WOULD SERVE

HER TRUE WELFARE

FOREWORD

This book is not homogeneous. But neither is life, not missionary life in India, anyway.

It presents a human India, in all sorts and conditions and moods, and a human being—recognized by her people, I hope, as a friendly one—moving amongst them. If it has been impossible to avoid seeing flaws and even serious lacks—what country or nation is without them? That love and sympathy underlie all that has been written will, I hope, be perceived by the reader.

The student of modern politics may look in vain for direct light on the present situation in India. Possibly, between the lines, he will find a little enlightenment.

At all events, all incidents, conversations with people, etc., are personal first-hand experiences; every person mentioned was met as presented. The descriptions in Chapter XVIII are quoted from the original letters of the Indian writer. The villages mentioned in the chapter on Outcastes I have all visited; the stories related were told me by eye-witnesses. For the rest I have not been dependent on memory; the material has been collected partly from letters carefully preserved by the lifelong friend to whom they were addressed, partly from notebooks, kept—to my present regret—only irregularly during the thirty-three years spent in India.

If—by presenting not theories, or abstract general pronouncements, but actual individual people—these pages contributed in the smallest degree to make this great country of infinite potentialities for good and for blessing the human race better understood and better loved—if they evoked in anyone the wish and the resolution to serve her, it would be great reward.

My thanks are due to the Editor of *World Dominion* for his courtesy in allowing me to embody two articles of mine published in his magazine in Chapter XVII; also to the L.M.S. managers of the Livingstone Press for permission to include "Winniamma," printed by them in the "Adventurer" series as a separate leaflet, now enlarged, in Chapter XV.

M. L. CHRISTLIEB

OXFORD
October 1930

CONTENTS

UPHILL STEPS IN INDIA

CHAPTER I

IN CAMP

When the idea of women missionaries going to villages was first proposed our Committee met it with unfeigned opposition.

"It is too rough for you."

"In the district one cannot avoid getting into holes. And when a woman gets into a hole she sits down and cries."

"Do you want to do a man's work?"

"No, a woman's," I replied, with the inherited meekness of a sex that through long ages has had to gain its points as best it could. (In my case, I admit, the said meekness breaks forth only at intervals.) "Aren't there women in the villages?"

That point, cunningly insisted on, could not be contradicted; and—in any case, they were really very reasonable and sympathetic. Though something of the feeling remained, "Well, if you come to grief don't blame *us*!"

Oh, their prophetic souls! Recently I had cause to think of their kindly warnings.

My tent had been pitched under the great banyan-tree near a little country railway station. Camp was to be struck and moved into the Hinterland farther from civilization by faithful Erana, while I rushed to Andapur by the morning train for stores and letters, returning at midday.

I was idly gazing out of the window of my little third-class compartment on the return journey, at the stopping place midway. There were another ten miles to go before I need stir. I heard the guard blow his whistle.

What was that apparition my startled eyes perceived trying to climb the spiked and barred station gate, waving arms and tearing a loin-cloth on a spike in the effort to get over quickly? Erana, by all that is untoward! What is he doing here? Why, I *knew* he was eighteen miles away in the new camping-place, my eyes must be lying. . . . But they were not lying; he was here, they insisted—so he could not be there—my bewildered brain moved at last. "Guard!" I shouted, hanging out of the window.

The train had already begun to move. But the guard on the platform caught my eye and my cry as the carriage slid past him and saw the frantic appeal; his red flag shot up as his whistle went again; the train stopped. Hastily I scrambled out with my belongings. The train went on.

"What has happened? Where is the tent?" I cried.

"The army! the British army! they have taken everything!" wailed poor Erana.

By degrees I elicited the facts. A British regiment from the North was marching to Bangalore. The road passes not far from my late camping-ground. Erana had packed everything and gone off to the village for the cart, leaving a coolie in charge.

At that very time the regiment marched past. Someone spied the bundles under the banyan-tree and, thinking they might be army stuff, went to inquire. The village coolie knew better than to risk an encounter with the British soldier, who is known to get angry very quickly when he is not understood. The lengthiest explanations would be of no avail. They always ended in an enraged Tommy shouting, "If you give me any more of your *bolo*[1] I'll put that in your *dekko*[2]!" The coolie fled.

So what looked like an officer's camp outfit, tent, table, chairs, suitcase, etc., was left unguarded under a tree. Word was passed along the line to the Colonel himself.

Some scamp of a cart-driver has thrown down his load

[1] Hindustani for "speak."
[2] Hindustani for "see."

and bolted, thought the officer. "Load it all up and bring it along," he ordered helpfully.

When Erana returned the place was empty. The affrighted coolie returned and told his tale. The dust of the regiment was disappearing along the white road. Erana did the most sensible thing he could and ran after them, all the ten miles to this station, where he arrived in time to extract me from the train. That was fortunate, anyhow.

"They are camped here, near this very station," he reported further. So in that respect also things might have been much worse. But the time to feel grateful was not yet. I was still too busy execrating the army and all its works.

"I must find the Colonel," I said, and thought of all the things one might say to him.

The station master and other station staff who had been listening with deep interest to the recital of a fellow creature's woes (which, as Emerson truly remarks, are by no means sources of unhappiness to others), now came forward helpfully.

"Officers are encamped in the travellers' bungalow near the station."

Their heads and mine being full of army, "officers" suggested only regimental authorities to us. I marched to meet them.

The midday heat lay oppressively on the land. Dripping, dusty, I arrived. Deep silence reigned. The bungalow appeared to be in profound slumber; the doors were closed.

A *peon's* repose was interrupted and he went in search of his master. I waited in the veranda, plying my fan. Time passed. No one appeared. It was too bad to disturb people's siesta, I thought, but after all, I had been left without any refuge anywhere, my tent having been reft from me, I could now hear the murmur of voices inside, some sort of discussion seemed to be going on.

At last an Englishman in mufti appeared, and I began my tale of woe.

"We'd better find the Colonel," my listener suggested.

It turned out the three occupants of the bungalow were civil officers from elsewhere on a shooting expedition.

I apologized for having troubled them, but he most kindly insisted on accompanying me in my further search. I was thankful not to be alone in the street of tents we presently reached; in the great heat they all had their flaps rolled up to catch stray breezes and exposed inmates in every state of *déshabille* till I did not know where to look—though to judge from their stares, they did.

News evidently flew ahead of us; an orderly approached in haste. "The Colonel asks the lady to wait in the officers' mess-tent."

When the comedy of errors was explained he was most courteous and apologetic—also a little incredulous.

"Do you mean to say you travel about among the natives all by yourself?"

"They are a very friendly and polite people," I assured him; "there is never any trouble, I am quite at home with them."

"Well, I always said an Englishwoman could go anywhere," he asserted with a fine sense of British superiority. "I shall never hear the end of this," he added with a laugh. "You say even your box of clothes is among the things we took? The story will be all over the station. Would you like some tea? Orderly, tea!"

My little hill of difficulty was melting away before I had had time to sit down and cry. The occupants of the bungalow intended leaving by the night train and until then kindly vacated a side room for me.

In the friendly fashion of white people meeting in the wilds of India we dined together that night, all of us hard put to it for suitable clothes and eyeing one another's makeshifts with relief. They waxed confidential.

"When we heard your voice outside the bungalow at midday," related the senior, "we were all frightened."

"Of what?" I asked, amazed.

He would not specify. "Cunningham here positively cowered. 'I won't go,' he said; 'you go, you're senior, it's up to you.' But I did not particularly want to go either," he confessed with a twinkle.

Mr. Cunningham smiled. "Each of us conscious of episodes in the past and fearful of vengeance overtaking us here in the wilderness! Perhaps the point should not be pressed!"

Another man turned the tables on me. "How much a month do you pay your converts to keep them?" he asked.

"It varies," I replied gravely. "Anything from eight annas to two rupees a month."

They laughed. "You are not to be drawn."

It was refreshing to meet them, and yet, to tell the truth, I was less at home with these men of my own race than with Indian villagers. Was it the lack of background indicated by such questions as the one about converts? A background possessed by every Indian. Even the simplest, most ignorant, may be said to live his life *sub specie aeternitatis.* However engrossed in the struggle for daily bread, however shameless in crude begging or bargaining, the conviction that this world is *maya*, that the Invisible is the Real, is deep within him. Beloved India, unique in this respect among all nations upon earth!

Yes, I was happier in the village of Kottapalli the next morning, when a crowd of women pressed into Obalamma's courtyard after me—no difficulty in talking to *them*! One woman brought her girl baby, its head was covered with running sores, the hair clotted with dirt. Fortunately it was not vowed to some god, which would have prevented anyone but the temple barber dealing with it; I was allowed to cut it all off, and to wash and anoint the little head and bandage it, at which its owner wept bitterly. The little first-aid case is very handy in the villages; another child was brought with the same trouble and treated similarly. My reputation was spreading, for now they came with a little motherless thing—said to be twelve months old but looking scarcely two. "It won't take milk."

I sat for half an hour in that village street, slowly getting a cupful into it by tiny spoonfuls; bottles, of course, are unknown, and it's as well, they would never be kept clean.

Village babies require all sorts of attention. "Why don't you cut its nails?" I asked, after the milk performance.

"We don't know how."

Well, I suppose I should not either, if I had no scissors. "Shall I do it?" I offered.

And the operation was performed amidst a silent group of spectators; silent with admiration of such skill, I fondly hoped, till I remembered that the cutting of nails as well as of hair is the prerogative of the barber, and barbers are by no means high caste. I had probably been sinking in their estimation all the time. Anyhow, the baby's little hands were no longer like claws, I consoled myself.

Wavering self-confidence received timely reinforcement. A man who had been listening while I talked to the women came forward and sat down in front of me.

"Do you want something?" I asked.

"Nothing at all."

His action of proximity, however, spoke louder than words, and I waited as patiently as I might.

"Nothing at all," he repeated presently, "only this. If you would speak to the *Reddi* for me. The man whose property is next to mine is withholding land from me. I fear he is bribing the *Reddi*. I am a poor man, I cannot give bribes. You are a great one, if you would speak to the

Reddi it would be better than bribes," and much more in the same strain.

"I fear I cannot," I replied. "But may I tell you a story? Many years ago there was a man like you, in the same trouble, all about his land. It was his brother who caused the quarrel. When a great *Guru* came to his village this man asked him to interfere. Behold, thus it was written: 'O *Guru!* tell my brother to divide the inheritance with me.' But the *Guru* said that was not his work. Nor is it mine. Would you like to know what else the *Guru* said?"

They would. Time passed.

"We must go to the fields now," said the women; "we like to listen to you, no one teaches us such things. But how shall we remember? You have told us a lot; but when you have gone how shall we keep our minds on it?"

"You come and teach wisdom," said a shepherd woman, "and for two or three days there is great joy in our hearts because we have learned a new thing; but then our work is all round us, it is easy to forget."

"But the earth is all round you too, and over all is the sky; when you see it remember who made it. And then pray, 'God who made earth and heaven, help me.' Will you do this?"

"To think of divine things is so difficult, said Obalamma; "our minds are on this and that, and to fix them on the heavenly way is very hard."

And very hard also is it to make them understand that faith is not the trained mental discipline of the ascetic wrapped in continuous meditation, but the childlike and practical basing of one's daily life on the fact of God, expecting from Him the help we need in our struggles and our sorrows and our common tasks. Is not that what Christ revealed when He went about in villages long ago saying

[1] Religious teacher.

the kingdom of God was near, the Rule of God very much nearer to men and women than they had thought?

And how desperately is that revelation needed here in India, with her ceaseless consciousness that she ought to find God and fix her mind on Him!

"We have no time to practise the way of *yoga*; but what you say is good, come again soon and teach us more," they said in friendly parting.

I walked on a couple of miles to the next village, where the tent was to be pitched. But the carts had not arrived. Had there been an upset among those rocky hills through which I had come?

As I went through the lanes of the village people stared, but soon recognition dawned.

"Missiamma has come," remarks buzzed about.

"Salaam, Mangamma, you are well?" I greeted an acquaintance coming round a corner.

"When did you come?" the woman asked in surprise.

"Now, this minute."

"But how?"

"I walked."

"Then come and sit down in my house and rest," said the neighbourly soul. Her verandah had been freshly floored with cowdung, fortunately a corner was dry. Immediately I sat down people crowded round.

"Where did you walk from?"

"Potukonda."

"Oh, poor thing, all that way? And alone, too. Why do you not ride on a horse when the Government give you all that money?"

"They give me none," I interpolated.

"No, she is not of the Government people," said a wise-acre, "she has come for our *Pirlu* festival."

"No, she has not," asserted a better-informed one, "the white people have no *Pirlu* god at all."

"Have they not? Really, Missiamma, is that true? Have you no *Pirlu*[1] god?"

"I tell you, they have not," the first speaker asserted again; "they worship the sun."

"Neither the sun, nor *Pirlu Swami*," I forced a word in edgewise, "but God who made heaven and earth."

"And no other *Swami* at all?" they asked in wonder. "Just God?"

"Yes, one God, the Father of us all."

"But how then do you get names for your children?" inquired a perplexed polytheist. "We call our children by the names of our gods. If you have only one how do you manage? There might be three or four children in a family."

This disability of monotheism had not occurred to me. "We have other names for them," I began, but the questioner's attention was turned by the arrival of a lusty boy between three and four years of age. He searched for his mother among the group and impatiently pulled at her cloth. Obediently she sat down. The boy pushed aside her jacket and began to suck at her breast. After a moment or two his hunger was satisfied and he ran away again. This being a common occurrence (for women often go on nursing children for three or four years) no one took any notice; but perceiving my interest the mother began to talk about the child.

"He was so ill when he was small. We took him to Tirupati and had his head shaved, both his and his sister's;

[1] *Pir* is Hindustani for "holy man." *Lu* is merely the Telegu plural form. This festival is one commemorating certain Mohammedan warrior saints in whose honour spears and tridents are placed in the mosques. On the last day these are taken out in noisy procession to fields or groves where ceremonies are performed.

In South India, Hinduism has adopted this festival and made it into one of idol worship, the spears, etc., being the idol which is honoured by the name of *Pirlu Swami*. (*Swami* = idol, god.) Thus accommodating is the Hindu Pantheon.

each child cost sixteen *duddu*,[1] and something for the barber besides. And we changed his name. So he was all right."

Evidently her thought was that the goddess of death was after the child, but was successfully hoodwinked by a shave and change of name into mistaking him for someone else.

"I name the Name," said an old man, "daily I say, Narayana, Narayana!"

"I want a horse very badly," interrupted a more worldly-minded one, "please give me one. Then I will remember your name every day."

"Give me but a little rice every month," requested a woman, "and I will follow you, your religion is good."

"Please sit over there now," hinted Mangamma. "I am going to whitewash that corner."

I moved. "Are you not going to do the whole?"

"No, this will do, it is enough for this festival."

Perhaps she had a lingering feeling that *Pirlu* was a Mohammedan feast originally, so she as a Hindu need not be too lavish with her whitewash.

Loud tomtoms drowned further talk. The *Pirlu* beggars had arrived, the noise close at hand was deafening; they looked at me expectantly.

"I do not carry money," I said, "so I cannot give you any. Please, would you beat your tomtoms a little farther off?"

The people around smiled compassionately. You were scarcely a "great one" if you did not give. But they made allowances.

"Poor thing, her carts have not arrived, she has nothing."

The children now became pressing.

"Will you go and see if my carts have come?" I tried to deflect their attention.

"We do not understand your words," said the resourceful

[1] *Duddu* = 4 pie. 12 pie = 1 anna, or the sixteenth part of one rupee.

ones, their bird in the hand—a strange spectacle in front of them—evidently being worth more than problematic arrivals in the bush.

I took no further notice, people drifted away. The life of the village flowed quietly past me. I pulled some paper out of my pocket and began to write. The children at first watched with interest, but it soon palled.

"She said, 'Go and see if the carts have come,' let us go and look," they resolved on trying new pastures.

Shouting with importance they returned running. The carts had been sighted.

I left the friendly people and walked towards the tamarind grove, half a mile along the river-bed. The sand was so hot that it burned my feet through my shoes; my feet became sorer and sorer as they sank into the loose burning sand, well trampled by the cattle. "Shall I ever get there," I wondered, "before I am roasted right through?" Perseverance in waddling brought me there at last.

"The road was so bad," Erana excused the late arrival, "the things were all shaken about; the lantern-box upset, I saw the oil leaking from the cart, we had to stop and repack everything."

"Get the cartmen to lend a hand now," I urged.

They usually help willingly in holding the ropes while the tent poles are pulled up, but these were new men, hastily commandeered by the military people that morning.

"It is not our caste, we cannot touch your ropes," they objected.

Nothing we could say availed to overcome that prejudice. "Certainly caste is the most vicious institution on the face of the globe," I thought resentfully, standing hot and hungry in the broiling midday.

At long last other help was obtained from more neighbourly-minded men in the fields, and two o'clock saw me safely inside a stifling hot tent.

But troubles were not over. A deputation from the village arrived.

"Please move your tent; under this tree we always put up the spears at the *Pirlu* festival, it is our custom."

But the camel refused to have its back broken by this last straw.

"It is too much trouble to take the tent down and put it up again," I objected firmly. "There are many trees in this grove. Put the *Pirlu* under another one."

"But it is our custom to have *Pirlu* under this one."

"Then change the custom for once."

"What can we do?" they murmured dejectedly.

The tent stayed where it was. It might have been Madame Tussaud's, the way it attracted sightseers. All the afternoon they came and went. One woman sat there for hours; she was mad, they said; all her jewels, worth thousands of rupees, had been stolen; the grief over this had made her go out of her mind. Poor soul. She brought me flowers and fruit and looked at me wistfully, no one could persuade her to go home.

A man passed, seemingly bent on business. But not his was the Western complaint:

> "What is this life, if full of care,
> We have not time to stand and stare?"

He had time for both.

"Are you looking for something?" I asked at last.

"Yes, I am looking for my cow," he said unexpectedly.

"And do you think she is under my chair?"

"No, I do not think she is under your chair. I like looking at you, you are not of our people."

Sancta simplicitas. I felt rebuked. His manners were better than mine. Was he not treating me with grave sincerity, while I . . . ? O recording angel, please make excusing dots too!

The evening and the morning brought their usual avocations in the villages. Returning from a neighbouring one the next midday I found my quiet grove invaded by pandemonium. The spears had been brought as close to the customary spot as possible, to the tree within a yard of my tent. There they were, stuck against an orange-coloured cloth which flamed in the sunlight, over them—O humourless East!—a battered Western umbrella was fixed; in front of them sat the musicians, loudly, ceaselessly, belabouring their tomtoms. Boys and youths were dancing rhythmically and gracefully behind them, and a countless multitude of people surrounded them, all in festive and noisy mood, ready for any fray. My advent provided the next one, the whole crowd of spectators swayed towards me. I had a sudden feeling as if a monster were upon me and fled into the tent, where for the moment they did not venture to follow. Those merciless tomtoms continued all day without a break. Presently Mangamma came to see me; seeing an Indian woman enter the tent the crowd took heart of grace to flood in after her, till I was pressed against the back wall of the tent, bewildered by the mass of eyes. With infinite trouble I persuaded them to depart, promising to come out presently.

A hasty cup of tea was swallowed. "The potter women want to see you," announced Erana. I went out to the shade of a tree a little farther from those maddening tomtoms. The potter women indeed had come, but were lost in the crowd which immediately rose upon me like a tidal wave; I felt rather like a submerged island. My personal taste would always prefer a quiet group in a veranda, and I rather wished for a magic wand enabling me to change the situation round me into that—but no such wand being handy, one had to do the best one could. After all, though they closed me in on every side, they were a very friendly crowd and quite willing to listen; in spite of the tomtoms tuning up with extra vigour they would not move till my throat was dry and my voice completely gone. Later on I found myself back in the tent, stared at by consecutive groups, while a man rushed wildly up and down the grove, flinging his arms about and shouting, "We are all fools, all fools! They [pointing to the tent] speak words of righteousness, but we are fools, all fools!"

The sun went down at last, the *Pirlu* were taken away, the people dispersed towards the river-bed. The infinite, unspeakable blessing of silence and of solitude descended upon the forsaken grove.

I fell asleep on my camp-cot; my brain still busy with nightmarish dreams. Without, the night sank down; the clouds also, the sun had set in ominous splendour, unheeded either by Erana or me. Down, down, came the rain.

I started suddenly from sleep. Something had run down my back. Were the crowds still jostling me? I thought drowsily, my consciousness clinging obstinately to its deep stratum of sleep. Something down my back again! Things moving, creeping, are not to be disregarded in the tropics, where snakes, scorpions, tarantulas, and their ilk, are always near neighbours. I was wide awake now. Again that sensation down my back. But now I distinguished it, ice-cold drops of water falling on me. Whence? The dim light of the lantern showed me the side of the tent aslant, leaning heavily and wetly against my mosquito poles and dripping on me as I lay. Outside I heard the heavy splash of rain. I shot out of bed, thinking to move the cot away from the wet tent wall. My wits were not at their best at that sleepy moment. For the instant I dragged the cot away the tent wall came after it. The iron rods holding up the net had been the last stay against disaster. The whole tent moved now. For in the hurry of that midday the pegs had been driven in hastily and superficially in hard ground; in the rain-sodden earth they had given way, the wind blowing against the wet canvas easily loosened them further, to my dismay I saw the main poles upholding the whole tent falling sideways. I should have rushed out while I could, but it only occurred to me to raise my arms and try and hold up the sinking concern. Quite useless, of course. I could not endure the weight for more than a minute or two, then my trembling arms were forced down, the weight descended on my shoulders now. A line of Schiller's flashed through my mind:

"*Ach unglüksel'ger Atlas, ich!*" [1]

as I stood under the mountain. For the weight, trebled by wet, of a large tent with an inner and an outer roof, each of threefold thickness of stout tent cloth, is prodigious. It was beyond my bearing anyhow. I was forced down, down. I grasped at the table in my descent, that also gave way; but somehow it served to save me, in another moment all the space left me in the world was a little three-cornered cavity formed by the camp-table at my back holding the weight of the tent off me to the extent of its width, about two feet. It gave me room to breathe anyhow, and I put the chance to good use by unearthly screams for Erana, so weird and loud that they penetrated even into his slumbers. I heard him pattering out from the kitchen tent. When he perceived in the darkness in place of an upstanding, well-behaved tent a flattened-out mass of damp misery he set up a wail, thinking for sure I was killed. But he was soon reassured by an angry command issuing from under that strange heap, "Stop that howling! lift up the cloth and let me get out!"

He lifted and I crawled, emerging into the night wearing the thin garment of tropical nightgear which, after the wormy passage through those wet tunnels, had not a dry shred in it. There I stood; the rain was still falling.

[1] "Oh miserable Atlas, I!"

"Strike a match, Erana, and let me see the time." It was two o'clock, but at the moment the flickering light deceived me, I misread it for four. In a little over an hour it will be light, I thought, startled; people will come, and —heavens, I had no clothes!

"You must crawl in, Erana, and find my things somehow," I urged, holding up the wet mass as well as I could; after repeated voyages of discoveries in the unseen the faithful one emerged with various oddments, a sopping skirt, a bedraggled blouse, and joy! a blanket. Also wet through, of course, but anyway, some sort of opaque cover. Now I could think of the next need. "Can you boil the kettle, Erana?" He departed.

Carts had been ordered for an early start next day and stood in readiness in the grove. I climbed into one, woke the driver and told him I must leave now as I had nowhere to stay, the tent would be too heavy to move till it was dry and that would take a day or two.

With the miraculous capacity of Indian camp servants, Erana presently produced steaming tea, also found me shoes and stockings and a pulped topee. I left him to follow with the tent when he could and bumped away into the night, hoping to reach the railway station in time for the morning train.

Then my mistake about the time became apparent. The night remained black. The driver missed the track. No star appeared. The cart swayed here and there—boulders, holes landing us again and again within an ace of destruction. But the rain stopped. Forthwith I hung my skirt and blouse outside, to dry as we proceeded, the blanket serving me meanwhile. We passed a solitary hut.

"Go in and ask them the direction to the road, please." The driver did, but within five minutes after leaving the hut we had lost it again. Bumping, jolting, shaving an upset every other minute, we continued, not knowing whither.

Ha, a thorn-hedge! that meant an enclosure of sorts, for sheep or a garden, and there is always a watchman. "Go, and ask them the way."

But the man came back from a fruitless quest. "They say they are asleep, they will not show, they will not believe my word."

Mahomet now bestirred himself to go for this mountain. The dark is full of demons for Indian villagers, very likely voices from outside in the night only proved their sinister presence near this solitary dwelling. Can I manage not to be mistaken for a devil, I thought, as I tapped my way round the thorn-hedge to the entrance.

"From Andapur, we!" I called reassuring greeting to suspicious faces, successfully counteracting by familiar phrase what might have been the effect of the blanket, still serving as dress, but certainly not what the white people usually wore, and for all the lonely gardener knew, quite a modish dress for a demon.

A slowly lightening East helped. By the time we were back at the cart light was rapidly devouring the sky. We could not miss our way now to the *estayshun*. And the station really hove in sight some hours after. I hauled down my flags at the sight and put them to their usual use of garments. But the morning train had gone.

So it meant waiting for the evening one. Food caused no perplexity; a station porter who kept fowls sold me some eggs and boiled them for me; the stationmaster's wife, a Brahmin, who, I daresay, does not often have white people come begging to her door, bestowed on me a plate of steaming rice and would accept no payment. In the goods-shed, on some sacks of grain, I made up for the disturbed night.

In the afternoon, radiantly golden after the rain, I wandered out into a green wilderness of little hills. It was indescribably beautiful among them; I left the footpath and climbed a little hillock to look over the shining earth. A delicate green mist seemed already to lie over yesterday's bare ground. I sat down in the shade of a big cactus; a red coppersmith bird flashed past me, wild pigeons cooed loudly all round. . . . Well, perhaps better return for the train now, I thought, and went leisurely back towards my foot-path. Alas, it had disappeared! One cactus-bush looked like another. I had taken no particular heed of direction as I had not come far. "I'll climb that hill," I thought, "then I can see the station." But the top of that hill only revealed similar little hills around. "That rather higher one over there must show it," I thought again, and, getting slightly nervous about time, ran hastily towards it.

In mid-career I stopped dead. One foot poised in air remained poised in air. A movement had caught my eye, a stealthy, soundless movement under that very foot. The ground seemed to be moving—no, it was a python. One of those enormous rock-snakes, twenty to twenty-five feet long, in colour matching the ground, had been sunning itself motionless in the wilderness till the sound of my approach had caused it slowly to glide towards its home. The complete cessation of sound—for I remained transfixed—caused it also to cease from activity. So there we were, the huge rock-snake under my foot, its horrid length apparently reaching to the horizon. What should I do? There is some tradition that one ought to kill snakes. What with? I had an umbrella, but the exigencies of camp life had deprived it of its latter end. The python looked rather tough. Drop a stone, then, and break its spine? But I never could hit anything, I might only irritate the creature, and the thought of fleeing through the wilderness with an angry python after me turned my joints to water. They were giving way as it was. I must have made a movement or some noise, the huge snake mobilized again and slid slowly past me. On, on, more and more length of snake disappeared under a boulder. Will the hole hold all of it? I thought anxiously, and it did. So there was an empty landscape again, only sinuous disturbances in the grass and sand showed where it had been too full a moment ago. The boulder looked innocent and dreamy in the sun, but I knew its horrid secret, and suddenly all the innumerable boulders around took on a malignant aspect. Each held the same horrid secret, without a doubt. How dreadful is this place, I thought, fleeing nervously towards that higher hill.

Then something shot up violently against my leg. Another python! and under my skirt already! I yelled and leaped several yards into the air, then glanced fearfully backwards. Nothing more than a long dry branch could be seen, I must have trodden on the front end, thus causing the back one to rise and hit me from behind.

What were those green parrots saying? Was all the jungle laughing? No more wilderness for me for the moment, thank you! Though I despise civilization often enough, at that minute it became the goal of my dreams; and no Greeks cried more enthusiastically, *Thalatta, Thalatta!* than I, reaching breathlessly the summit of the desired hill and sighting the ugly corrugated iron roof of the goods-shed, panted rapturously, "The station, the station!"

CHAPTER II

AN AFTERNOON IN HINDU HOMES

"EVERY life takes courage to live," I read somewhere recently, in Brierley, I think, and wherever I turn I find it illustrated. India resembles another Eastern country in this regard; in the pages of the Gospels one is confronted constantly by human need, sickness, sin, grief of many kinds; the people Christ met always seemed in desperate need of help. He could always give it—while we . . .? Take to-day.

I heard that Rama Reddi had died; as I know the family I went to see them. I was received with loud wailing and weeping. The mother's tears flowed the whole time, though to judge from her words part of her grief seemed to be due to the poverty that was now upon them.

"We have a debt of three thousand rupees!" This with a heartbroken sob. "We shall have to go and beg!"

The widow's younger sister stood near her; she wore a pretty *sari* and had all her sister's jewels on. A flower-seller came to the door. The mother haggled with her, then bought a few ounces of blossoms. (Flowers, the heads of jasmine or marigolds ready strung on thin thread for twisting in the hair, are sold by weight in Indian bazars.)

"For whom are they?" I asked.

"For the little one, of course," said the mother. "What have we"—touching herself and the elder girl—"to do with flowers now?"

The little widow—herself still young—turned away. I had never seen her without ornaments and flowers before.

A *Bogum*[1] woman came in. Her hair had all fallen out and she hoped I knew a remedy. "Come to my house," she begged, "my little girl comes to your school "

[1] Caste of prostitutes.

In her courtyard she told me something of her story. She was first kept by a Brahmin to whom, she asserted, she had given all her money and property. Later on he left her and is now in Bangalore. My little schoolgirl is her adopted child. I shivered. Adopted, for what purpose?

"If she is not your own daughter I beg you to let Papamma come to me," I implored.

"You must ask her father" (i.e. the man with whom she is now living).

A bigger girl whom she called her niece was sitting by. Too late to save her, I could see. Little Papamma had come running in and sat near us, listening to all that was said with a grave little face. Though only about ten years old the meaning of the whole conversation was perfectly plain to her.

The thought of child tragedies in India drives one almost mad at times.

But it is the hardest thing to effect a rescue. Evince an interest in an individual case and immediately the person is spirited away. The walls of caste close solidly against you.

Some time ago I went to see a merchant woman. Dorcas was with me. The woman was not in her private house, but had gone to her shop in the bazar street. Dorcas went to call her. I sat in the courtyard and waited. A young girl came out of the house and sat down picking over vegetables.

I started talking to her and found she was the merchant's niece and alas! a widow. She had come from the village where she lived with her father and brother, to visit her aunt in this town.

"And I am very afraid," she said urgently. "My father is an old man, my brother is married and has a family to keep. Will he want to look after me when my father dies? Where shall I turn then?"

She looked pitifully young. I urged her by all means to keep straight.

"If anyone tempts you to do wrong run away to me. You must be seventeen or eighteen; at eighteen you are of age, you can do as you like. If you don't want to do wrong no one can compel you. I promise to receive you any time you come."

The girl asked eagerly for names and the position of the Mission house. While I was explaining these the aunt returned and seemed by no means pleased to find me alone with the girl, whom she sent immediately into the house. Next day Dorcas tried to see her again; the visit was "not convenient." She went again a few days later; the girl was said to be out. Again, later still, she "had gone back to her village." No inquiries or messages since have enabled Dorcas or myself to get a glimpse of that girl again.

In the case of the *Bogum* woman adopting Papamma it was presumably the desire to provide for her old age by the girl's future earnings; in the merchant's family a similar motive would operate, the wish not to be burdened with the lifelong support of a widow. Money considerations in either case. The young widow would—by plainly showing her that she was a burden—practically be pushed to accept the precarious position of someone's easily discarded mistress; the poor child foresaw this. Hinduism would connive at this; but the suggestion to let a caste widow go to the Christians would rouse the fiercest opposition, for it would mean that unforgivable thing: breach of caste.

India holds tenaciously to caste. Yet, seeing how cruel it is in some of its results, caste will have to go.

I seem often to come upon tragedies; but, of course, in individual households they are not always at tragedy point. Their lives are dull and ordinary mostly, and yet, however much they seem so on the surface, they are in reality neither dull nor ordinary. Is any life, ever?

An old schoolgirl invited me to come in and see her people. A strange woman sat among them, with a hard, set face.

"Who is she?" I asked. "I have not seen her with you before."

"One of our relations," replied my pupil's mother.

"Living here? How is it I never met her?"

"No, not living here. We did not speak to her for years."

"Why was that?"

"Quarrels. She wanted us to give her three thousand rupees' worth of jewels and property. She said it was her share. We refused. She went to law. And all was lost in the expenses of the case, the disputed money and more of my daughter's and son-in-law's, and all her own. So now she has nothing."

"Then do you feed her?"

"Ram, Ram, should we feed her when she made us lose all that money?"

"Then how does she live?"

"She takes care of the sick child of the goldsmith people."

A poor, emaciated little thing said to be two years old, but looking hardly six months, was held out for my inspection. I looked at its nurse, who told me her name was Rajamma. Her hard face troubled me. I made an attempt to reach her.

"Rajamma, there are greater treasures than money. Even now they are waiting for you."

She looked at me unmoved, slightly shook her head, then picked up the wailing child and went out. The emptiness of her inner world descended like a weight on my own spirit.

Inside the half-open door I saw a young man sitting on the floor, busily writing.

"My son-in-law," explained the mistress of the house.

"What is he writing?" I asked.

"He is writing a million times 'Rama, Rama, Sri Rama.'"

"What for?" I asked, astonished.

"To gain merit," she explained.

I remember having read the Indian story of a man who was a great sinner naming his son Rama. When he was about to die the angels of *Yama*, the god of death, were waiting to take his soul to hell, as soon as it should leave his body. The sick man called to his son, "Bring me a little water, Rama!" Just then he died. The merit of having said the name of the god at the last was so great that his soul was taken to *moksha*, heaven, instead.

I had read it as a fantastic fairy story; but here I saw how the idea behind it was woven into the very heart and life of the people. The pity of it, the waste of it! There the young man sat and wrote and wrote. . . .

But perhaps the zeal and devotion, or the anxiety which prompted the writing, will not fail of some response?

A visit to a Brahmin family came next. They were new people and I had planned to make friends with them by bringing bits of fancy-work which had been welcomed and asked for in other houses. But the ladies looked askance at the little mats for embroidery, caste fears rose; were these things for Brahmins to touch? They were evidently afraid to handle them; I pocketed them again in embarrassed haste. Conversation, however, was easier than it often is on first visits; they were very intelligent, asked eager questions about Japan and Russia and the relations of these countries to England, etc.

What amazed me in that household, so pious and orthodox, so well educated, were the pictures hung close beside one another along one wall, about a dozen. They represented mythological stories of a scarcely decent kind. How these gentle and modest women could endure them I could not think. They were so unpleasantly obtrusive that I could not keep my attention off them. "Those pictures," I stammered, failing to catch a remark.

Unembarrassed, they told the story of one. A certain saint, tempted to evil by a heavenly houri.

"But do you think it is helpful to have that story continually recalled to you?'

"Oh, but it was not wrong. You see the houri came from heaven."

"But that one," I objected, pointing to a worse picture.

They seemed to see it with my eyes for a moment, but soon reverted to their habitual mode of thought.

"It is different when a god does it," they explained.

I felt I had come upon a bedrock of Hindu mentality fatal to true progress. There are no moral absolutes in India. Everything can shift and shift again. When morality is divorced from religion, and again religion from daily life, where shall we find a foothold?

I am constantly meeting these pictures and always hear the same explanation. The lack of logic that has so often surprised me in Hindu minds has religious roots, the toughest and strongest of any. The magnitude of the task of replacing ideas of different moral standards for gods and men by one of the majesty of moral Law, of substituting true Absolutes for false ones, when false ones are embedded in the loyal and conservative hearts of Indian women, appals me.

I know it is true that in the West also, indeed throughout the history of the Jewish and Christian religions, qualities were attributed to God that were shocking to a later and finer moral sense. The difference is that at the time of their inception they were held to be just and right. As soon as the prophets—the advanced religious thinkers of any age—began to perceive the difference between their own highest moral sense and some popular orthodox conceptions of God, agony and conflict began, leading in the end to a higher idea of God. And it remains true that no comfortable way of staccato thinking may be permitted to any true follower of Jesus Christ.

Here in this Indian home these Hindu ladies were not defending immorality in itself, only immorality in the god. They themselves were better than their creed. When that happens is it not time for the creed to go?

From the Brahmin house I went to the small courtyard of friendly Sudra people. There was much coming and going at first; passers-by from the street looked in and joined the audience for a while and went out again; but one old man stayed on and listened steadfastly. Presently he burst forth:

"I act according to the sense God gives me. If He gives me the wisdom to follow your way I will join it. If He does not give it how can I?"

"Have you any sons?" I asked.

"Three."

"When they were small did you ever beat them for a fault?"

"Often."

But the inference was lost on him. Free will he had not

"If God moves me to do it I will do it; if He does not, what can I do? You say we must leave the evil and choose the good and believe in Him—let God move me to do all that. If He first does not work all this in me it would be vain for me to try," he persisted.

"What you say is true," I admitted. "It is taught in our religion also. *It is God who worketh in you both to will and to do.* But listen further. *Work out your own salvation. . . .*"

Some children ran in, holding young cholum-stalks. They sat down to gaze at me and started chewing their stalks.

"Do you like them?" I asked.

"They are sweet," a woman explained, "while they are so tender."

"I have never tasted them," I said, and turned back to the man.

"They are the gift of God, are they not?" pointing to the cholum-stalks. "We could not make them. But their taste is known only to these children. I, though I sit near and see them enjoy it, do not know the taste. Is it not the same with salvation? It, too, is the gift of God; it is not of ourselves.

But like these children have we not to lay hold of it and make it our own and thus learn its sweetness?"

But the old man did not really want new light; perhaps, also, he did not like his pronouncements not being taken as final. He got up and hobbled away.

Keshamma, the housewife, seated at her spinning-wheel, shook her head sagely. "No one can change their religion."

"The goldsmith makes many things," added another listener, "nose ornaments, armlets, necklaces, rings, there are many names of jewels, but all are gold. You and we say different names, but we all mean God."

"Then shall we think of Him together now?" I suggested, and started teaching them a lyric. In the very middle of it a man arrived holding out a necklace, a double string of thick corals. Keshamma stopped her spinning to take it and asked the opinion of the others. Lyrics were at a discount, we all crowded round to look at it.

"How much?"

"Eight rupees," said the vendor.

It was passed round amid whispers. "We offered six."

"He asked nine yesterday."

"Give it back," said the seller impatiently.

But the man of the house had come out. "Give it," he said briefly, and paid the man. He held out the necklace to his niece, a young married woman sitting in the background; "Here, tie it on."

She made no movement to take it; Hindu decorum, I supposed.

"Why this for me? I do not want it," she said, not even glancing at it.

"She wanted another more expensive one," Keshamma informed the rest of us. "She is pregnant."

It is supposed to be wise to give expectant mothers what they desire, and a necklace having been plainly hinted at, a necklace was bought. But as it was not the expensive kind the young woman continued to turn up her nose at it. The uncle grew tired of holding it out to her; an older woman came to the rescue and hung it round her own neck, for the time being, it was understood by all. But even temporary possession was not to be despised; she went out to show off the purchase to all her friends in the street. Much alike are the ways of women, East and West.

In the lane I met one of our Christians, a young farmer. "Please come home with me, we have a visitor."

I found a white-haired Hindu woman with a noble face sitting with his wife.

"She is my aunt, Pedda Subbamma," Giriappa explained. Giriappa himself and his mother are the only Christian members of a large Hindu family.

"You do not mind staying with Christians, Subbamma?" I asked.

"It is peace here," she answered simply. "I have suffered much. After my husband's death I brought up a nephew as a son. I had no children of my own. I got him married; there was a little child. I was happy for a while. But the nephew died, also the little one. Only my daughter-in-law remained. No one can know the evil of that woman. I cannot say how bad she was."

She paused. Her voice had taken on a note of deep sadness. Was her story merely the proverbial one of disagreement between mother-in-law and daughter-in-law? I noticed the deep lines on her face.

"Every kind of sin she did," the old woman went on mournfully, "even killing her unborn children. She raised her hand against me, as I grew older and weaker in body. She even struck me in the face. One evening she said I must go to the well with her. It was the large well in the fields. We went down the steps and she drew the water. Then she pointed to a sweet-smelling herb growing by the edge.

"Please pick me that," she said.

I did not suspect anything, but stooped to pick it. At that moment she gave me a great push and I fell into the water. It was dark and no one near. I rose to the surface and called out, 'O Father! O Lord Jesus! O Jesus Saviour!' for on my visits here I had heard of Him."

"Were you very frightened?" I asked.

"No, not frightened of death," she replied, "but I did think of my brother. He would inherit my property. Will they think he killed me, I wondered, and felt very afraid of that. I thought that must not happen. I struggled and struggled and must have got across the well along the bottom, for suddenly I felt the steps and climbed up."

"What happened at home?" I asked breathlessly.

"When my daughter-in-law saw me, she said: 'How clumsy you were to fall into the well. I was getting a rope to help you out.' There were no witnesses, I could not do anything. But I never felt safe again."

"So she will stay with us now," said Giriappa, and added in an aside to me, "and I think she will be a Christian soon."

"I am tired," said the old woman patiently. "I will go in and rest. It is good to have no fear."

"*Towards evening time there will be light.*" God grant it may be so for this brave and suffering spirit, I thought, as I cycled homewards and saw the west aglow.

Passing the compound of another neighbour, the English Collector's, I turned in there for a moment. He had recently brought a bride to his home.

"When I have unpacked my boxes and arranged all my things what is there to do in a place like this?" the bride had asked me when I first called. So I went in to ask how she was faring.

"Bored, as usual," she said. "I went out this evening, and saw the lights of the houses in the town extension. I thought how nice it would be if those were the lights of English bungalows."

"The Indian people too are very interesting," I ventured.

"But I am not a missionary. I could not talk to them about religion."

I also find it pretty difficult, often enough. But is it the only subject? It is true, there are many barriers to intercourse. The difficulty of language alone is hard to surmount, let alone a great many others, differences of customs, manners, tastes, as well as the rigours of officialdom. So I suppose English brides in quiet *mofussil* stations like this one must go on being bored. A merciful Providence is tempering the wind to this lamb by indicating that a baby is being sent along.

Meanwhile, like so many others in the town, this life also, in strange surroundings, in much inevitable loneliness, takes courage to live

CHAPTER III

BY HOLY RIVERS

I AM on my way to the strange North. A conference has been called on Mohammedan work in Lucknow. It was thrilling at the Junction this morning to see the great mails go by, *Delhi to Bombay, Bombay to Calcutta*, and to read such lovely titles as *Behar and Orissa Railway, Rohilkand Railway*. After our more clumsy southern names—for who is attracted at first sound by Ittekallipalli, Muntimadugu, Doddaballapura? —I repeated with endless pleasure, Rohilkand, Rohilkand!

The country glides past and the outlook from the windows is tugging at my heart. Meadows with the evening mist rising from them, fields with large trees dotted about; a crisp keen air; it might be England!

Lucknow. I arrived in the dark, so saw scarcely anything of the city as we drove through it, but when I reached the Mission settlement where I am lodged, behold it was an old palace of the kings of Oudh. In the Mutiny some Mission property was destroyed; in compensation this palace was given to them. I am in a room about twenty-four feet high; it is reached by odd passages round sudden corners. One door opens on a courtyard enclosed by a wall—was this the women's quarter? did they take the air on that grass plot? There are strange exits, hidden doors and stairs; I feel in a new world of intrigue and romance, or, rather, a very old one, and look longingly at the walls to tell me what they have seen. After dinner I did not join the multitude in the drawing-room, but went out into the starlit garden where presumably the old kings used to walk.

"Ere ever the ancient years had gone
With the old world to the grave,"

what had been thought and suffered in these very grounds by another race?

There are about forty delegates in this palace; interesting names are whirring round; people from Aden, Turkey, Palestine, Syria; and, withal, several bishops from India. It is enough to overawe a common missionary from the benighted South Indian plains.

The meetings last all day, but the early mornings are free. To-day some of us drove to the Residency, of the great historic association during the Mutiny. It was deeply moving to stand in the underground place where 260 English women and children were herded together from June till November. How did they exist, I wondered. In these cellars of the Residency light comes through ventilators let in on the level of the ground outside. This secured immunity from shells, though one managed to burst in; the place where it tore the wall is still visible. I walked away from my companions and stood alone with the past. Pillars and archways form divisions which allow of some privacy. But to think of the many children, cooped up here during the hottest months—and the uncertainty and fear before the mothers.

A baby was born here during the siege.

The grounds are immense, and the buildings in it many; how they could defend so straggling a place for months is a miracle. The battered and ruined Residency itself is perhaps the most moving place of any—the room where the shell wounded Sir Henry Lawrence; the house by the gate where he died; the banqueting hall turned into a hospital, the well from which, exposed to fire, they had to get their water.

I went up to the tower, its walls bespattered with the marks of shot and shell, where every day an officer was on telescope duty to mark the movements of the besieging forces; from there floats now, visible to all Lucknow and to many miles of country round, the Union Jack.

I leant beside the flagstaff and looked out over the land, marked the wide boundaries that were kept by that small force and wondered at human fortitude.

The cemetery was the last place visited; Sir Henry Lawrence's grave and others; among them that of a young wife barely twenty years old who died during the siege and lies there with her two little ones.

These memories are unhappy, say some. But is it not a truer view that blood and tears and suffering have created a bond between India and Britain that cannot easily be broken?

Next morning other sights of Lucknow drew us: tombs, mosques, palaces, built by the Mogul emperors; it is wonderful to anyone coming from the sunbaked mud huts of southern villages to see such magnificent erections—those Mohammedans could build! It has never been my happy lot to see the Taj, but even here, where their buildings are said to be decadent, I marvelled. What specially attracted me was unexpected and almost hidden grace; part of one palace, with slender fluted pillars shooting up, archwork and tracery showing fragile and visionary against the sky, looked like a fairy dream, yet I could discover no special reason for all this beauty, as it was hidden on a side wing where it served no purpose of pomp. Did they wish to express an idea of beauty, regardless of practical ends?

An hour or two before departure I fared forth into the modern city, not yet seen at all. A gari deposited us in the heart of the bazar. This was the India known from Mrs. Steele's books: over-hanging balconies on higher storeys, with trellised screens and lattice-work and faces peeping—or sometimes exposed boldly to view: which here in the North means that their owners are not respectable. One is thankful for the freer life in the South, where none but Mohammedans are *gosha.* In the street below, the crowd surged up and down, jostling us. There were many curious figures; the children much fairer than ours in the South; and instead of the scanty garments and even naked backs seen in our warm southern regions, almost everyone wore padded clothes; and indeed, it had turned fearfully cold, with a bitter north-east wind. We gazed into the booths and shops on either side; fruit-shops had apples from Kashmir, dates from Bassorah, walnuts and hazelnuts and other good things we never see in our bazars. Willingly I could have spent hours wandering about that fascinating Rialto; but trains are inexorable. And so, goodbye to Lucknow!

Benares. I am actually in the holy city of Hinduism and have watched its desperate intensity. My visit fell at a fortunate time; to-day is a special festival. Cold and dark notwithstanding, the pious bathing is done in the early morning. The sun was not yet over the trees when we arrived at the river. The streets leading to the water were crowded with pilgrims; thousands of villagers were flocking into the city. We moved with them to the water and at last I looked upon the stately Ganges. We chartered a boat and glided upstream in front of the sacred *ghats.* The sight made me hold my breath. As far as one could see, up the farthest of the wide flights of steps crowded a many-coloured multitude, wedged closely together, all pressing down to the water; the foremost actually in the water, the rest pushing forward in their craving to get to the cleansing river. Great precautions are taken by the British Raj to prevent the many drowning accidents which used to occur at times of religious exaltation, when the surging multitude at the back frenziedly pressed front ranks farther and farther out into deep stream; now a succession of railings in the water safeguards their devotions. We drew closer ashore to watch individuals; it seemed almost rude and intrusive; but every worshipper was too absorbed to take note of others. Men and women of all ages were dipping under the water; some three times, some six; murmuring, reciting, counting beads or fingers; here and there hands were raised high in supplication, or folded reverently below bowed heads. Moved in heart we watched these expressions of tireless search after the Unseen and the Incomprehensible; the dipping under the water surely signified the consciousness of the great need of purification; the hands stretched out and the eyes upraised seemed a mute appeal for help to see "a door opened in Heaven," nay, perhaps even a passionate plea to have the riddle of this weary life explained by the vision of Love and Sacrifice at the heart of the universe. *In the midst of the throne . . . a Lamb . . . as it had been slain.*

We drifted farther out in order to take in the whole magnificent sweep of bathing *ghats*, temples and palaces behind; going downstream we presently reached the burning *ghats*. A fresh pyre had been lit; naked feet protruded from the wrapped up corpse lying on it. It is not permitted now to throw bodies into the river; but ashes and garlands floated in the water round us. A little aside on a flight of steps in the shade of a temple sat a woman alone, weeping; at her feet on the lower step lay a shrouded shape. She was waiting her turn for a pyre, doubtless; her lonely figure on the steps, sunk in grief, knew nothing of to-day's festivity. No one heeded her or her sorrow. I wanted to get out and sit by her in silence; if perchance it were possible to convey to her, without words, the fact of a great sympathy in the Invisible. But the river took us on and she faded from sight, alone with her dead.

We floated down till we reached the chief mosque, where we climbed the minaret, a rather breathless ascent; but it rewarded us by a splendid view over the city and the river. Descending from the heights, we plunged into the alleys and gullies of the city. Here, too, beat a pulse of Benares. In the narrow passages between tall houses, leaving only strips of sky visible above, thronged festive crowds; sweetmeat sellers, garland sellers, and still more frequently, idol sellers, showed their wares at every corner; sacred bulls impeded progress in unexpected places where there was no room for them or anyone else.

The festival intensified no doubt the passion of worship in the air everywhere. It came to a head at "The Golden Temple." Here *pradakshanam* was being performed, i.e. sacred trees with idols leaning against them were circumambulated; not by ones and twos as I had often seen it in the South on ordinary days, but by crowds. Amongst the villagers I saw a Brahmin woman; she was so unwieldy she could hardly get along, but the fervour caught her; she reft up her *sari* to be able to step out, unconcernedly displaying stout limbs, and then footed it with the best round the tree. Again and again we came upon this ceremony; coins rained upon the *pujari*, the idol was smothered in garlands and drenched in scented water.

Near the entrance to the temple the crowd became so dense and pushing that we fled up some stairs beside a flower shop; the owner, being a friend of one in our party, permitted us to look from his balcony on the extraordinary sight below. A crowd outside was mad to get into the temple; a crowd inside mad to get out; it took my breath away to watch the pushing, fighting, jamming; so dense was the mass that I felt we could step from the balcony on to their heads and would never reach the ground. The one policeman in the gate was almost overwhelmed; presently the gate of an alley, whence the crowd was perpetually augmented, was closed; two or three more policemen stood guard over it. Still the swaying, hustling, pressing of the seething human mass below went on; turbans came off, women were lifted off their feet, children cried, garlands were flung about wildly, a mad frenzy to get in or out of the temple seemed to possess them all; our Benares friend, with her twenty-eight years in the city, said she had never seen the like. I could have stood on that balcony all day, but others had less time; by discreet backstairs and back alleys we wormed our way from the neighbourhood of the Shrine.

But not even in narrow lanes is one ever far from unexpected religious exhibitions. In another temple we saw a *guru* teaching a group of women; here and there streams of people were knocking their noses and foreheads against sacred stones, strewing flowers, flinging scented water, bestowing rice, offering coins—a reckless madness of devotion enflamed all minds. Wherever one walked, throughout the city the heart of Hinduism seemed to be throbbing with intensest life.

There are flaws, of course; the inevitable beggars, for instance; a more shamelessly begging place cannot exist! The devotee sits with crossed legs, mumbling prayers; you think him devout, but as you approach he shoots his hand out, "*bakshish*," murmurs the insistent voice; you stand and marvel at the hypocrisy. But not all are like this; there are many who do not see you, who look neither to the right, nor to the left; as far as appearance goes their minds are rapt. With more worldly minds ourselves, we went into the brass bazar, the silver bazar, the silk bazar, and I wished for the gold of Ophir to buy some of the beautiful things!

The afternoon found us at the Central Hindu College. A student courteously showed us over the boarding quarters, and the lecture halls; the grounds in the centre were ablaze with flowers and most beautiful; longingly I looked at the youths in the verandahs and garden—would that they might have the right ideals set before them! In the fine meeting-hall of the Theosophical Institution close by, pictures are hung impartially round the walls, of Christ, Mrs. Besant, Colonel Olcott, Madame Blavatsky, and others.

At the Monkey Temple we found nothing very remarkable save monkeys, rivalled in numbers by the beggars. The latter clustered round us, *pujaris*, priests, Brahmins, fakirs, all intimating their desire for *bakshish*. When one of them came rather too near, a man who already had a plate full of coins, I held out my hand to him with the beggar's gesture and said with the beggar's whine, "You might give us some, for a change." They do not know English, but they did not mistake the gesture and laughed and let us alone.

Behind the temple is a most lovely thing: a big tomb, like a temple, entirely carved in white marble; so delicate and transparent is the work in the doors and windows, which are all solid slabs of marble, that they are made to look like fragile lace. A Hindu saint lies buried there. When the heart of India is touched by Christ, when she pours out to Him her matchless capacity for devotion, what cathedrals will she erect?

The afternoon light was taking on a deeper gold as we went on to the riverside. To our right, as far as eye could see, meadows of tall green grass sloped gently to the water's edge; myriads of yellow flowers dotted them all over and shone like the heart of an English summer day. On the left the river in a wide semicircle seems to want to creep into the city and the city appears to embrace the river; behind us the sun was sinking; Benares lay bathed in the golden glow, indescribably beautiful. I went to a platform, built out over the water, where usually devotees would sit and meditate, but which was now deserted. Women came to bathe; prayers were muttered; I had lost myself in the lovely scene, but someone who did not approve of my sitting there broke the spell by bringing a mat to insert between my defiling bodily presence and the sacred boards which support willingly enough the mendicants' filthy rags.

We took a boat and floated out into the sunset. From the burning *ghats* the flames of three pyres made fiery paths across the shining water, weirdly illuminating the darkening shore. Temple bells were ringing; the tall grass reverently bent its head in the evening breeze; in the majestic sheet of water the clarity of the evening sky was perfectly reflected. Boats full of pilgrims were gliding past, we heard the chanting of prayers; garlands floated by now and then; faintly the temples were outlined in the fading light; softly, gently the day died on the bosom of the river. We drew ashore, and got out to see the most sacred spot of all, a well, supposed to have sprung from a drop of Vishnu's blood. We stood at the railing and looked down into the muddy water into which numbers of people were rushing for the sacred plunge. A priest kept his eye on each new-comer, demanding fees, and soon we also were assailed by demands for *bakshish*. "Why should we give?" we asked. "Because I am a Brahmin," was the unabashed reply. We turned back to the boat, and drifted amidstream to be alone with the quiet night and the beauty of the river. The stars came out, the flames from the burning *ghats* looked more wild and fantastic, till we rounded the curve and all faded from view save the great murmuring water and the mighty sky overhead.

And so good-bye to Benares, her spiritual passion and her earthliness, her hypocrisy, her devotion, her endless longing; queen of the Ganges, goal of a million hearts; yet with her own quest unended.

CHAPTER IV

DOMESTIC AFFAIRS

GENERALIZATIONS are nowhere more risky than in India; a dictum with which Sister Nivedita—whose book, *A Web of Indian Life*, I only recently got hold of—evidently did not agree. "The roseate hues of early morn" are much in evidence in her pages, which present an idealism gone rampant.

It so happened I was reading this highly-coloured book while staying in my friend Helen Powell's little rest-house, the last house of the main bazar street in Penuroy. At mid-day, in the upstair room whence I could overlook the street and all its happenings, I had just come to the glowing sentences where Hindu women are compared to the tall, chaste lilies too sacred for public gaze and set in the shrine of the sanctuary in modest retirement, sheltered from the world in their gentle innocence, as are the white flowers upon the altar.

At that very moment such a screeching din arose in the street that I rushed hastily to the window to see who was being murdered. But it was only two women in violent altercation. So high-pitched and shrill were their voices and with such lightning speed rushed the words that I could not follow all the abuse, but I made out that the cause of the quarrel was that one woman "for nothing at all" had caught hold of the child of the other and lifted it by its ears. "To you there is great sin this day!" shrilled the mother. Three times they separated and three times they returned to the attack, until neighbours interfered.

"Oh, Sister Nivedita, what do you say now?" I apostrophized the author.

What she would have said was that she was writing of the women she knew, *purdah nashin* ladies, probably Brahmins, in the North. And I am in the "benighted Presidency," where even Sister Nivedita might agree that some women, though neither poor nor low caste, do not suggest the sacred retirement of shrines, nor remind anybody of lilies.

Of course one immediately wants to qualify that statement. Indian womanhood possesses as much charm and dignity as do any Western representatives of the sex. Only the bazar turmoil, occurring at that moment, pointed, one must admit, to other realities besides Sister Nivedita's.

I returned to her book and proceeded to the chapter on marital relations. "What does the wife want with vulgar companionship? She is content to worship." "As a nun to the sanctuary she repairs to her shrine, fragrant with the name of her lord."

Does she, now, I thought. What about Sundaramma, a young Brahmin wife whom I met recently in the huts on the *maidan* (Andapur being evacuated for plague)—though her married home is in the very town I was visiting at that moment. Her story was that she endured being kicked and beaten by her husband for five years. Then she ran away to her parental home. Her father, however, is dead; I saw only an old grandmother. Negotiations for reconciliation were opened. The husband demanded not her return, but that of her jewels. He went to court with this demand. The court decided not to allow the jewels apart from the wife. She is still separated from him. Her account is that she will not return to him, also that he demands a thousand rupees before he will take her back. It sounded contradictory.

"You have been to see Sundaramma?" they said in another Brahmin family. "A young man of the *Bogum* caste visits at her house," they added significantly. Was that the explanation of Sundaramma's own tale of the husband's demand for a large sum before receiving her back?

Very likely; but what lay behind that? I heard the husband was ill-tempered. A wife is entirely at the mercy of her husband, brutal and cruel though he may be. Her duty, her religion, her hope of heaven, is to endure without complaint. One pictures it, a child given over to a man of bad qualities who has never learned self-restraint. If she disobeys —beatings, nay even burnings. (Such things have been reported in the papers and the courts.) Perhaps that was the beginning of Sundaramma's rebellion and subsequent undoing? If a cry for protection and for a little happiness arose, if an intrigue with a young *Bogum* man followed, is it to be wondered at? And then, if scandal and the contempt of women of her caste drove her again to seek reconciliation every advantage would lie with the man. Public opinion would back him throughout.

Indian married life holds many shadows, in spite of Sister Nivedita.

The conviction of women's inferiority has desperately deep roots. One comes upon them in all sorts of ways.

I entered a courtyard around which were the dwellings of several Lingait families. (The Lingaits are a numerous sect in South India and consider themselves in caste the equals of Brahmins.) A small separately built room stood in the middle of the large yard, whitewashed and clean. I caught a glimpse of a niche in the wall, and flowers and a lamp.

"Is it a little prayer-room?" I asked.

"It is."

"Do you go there when you have a little spare time to meditate and pray?"

General laughter answered me. "Why, we are not allowed inside."

"Then who goes there?"

"The men do."

"But don't you go with them to hand them the things for worship?" This is done in Brahmin houses.

"No, we are not allowed inside. Small girls may go, but not after they are of age."

We left the problem and, settling down on the steps of a

verandah, became interested in the teaching. Suddenly there was a flutter. Not a woman remained seated; some vanished into the house behind me, some passed out into the lane, in the twinkling of an eye my audience had melted away. I looked round to see the cause of the disturbance and beheld a Man! He stood in the doorway and in a lordly manner demanded milk.

What took me by the throat was my own violent impulse to stand up deferentially. Was it that I had been feeling so one with them that the mute command issued by the sudden masculine presence communicated itself to me also? Or was the new consciousness of sex equality in me a so recent racial acquisition that it was easily dislodged by a much older one? I found myself positively clinging to the verandah steps to prevent myself rising. Yet the intruder was only the head servant of a European in the station, come to ask for his master's evening milk. At that master's bungalow he would respectfully have risen at my arrival; here in the Indian household, among womenfolk, I very nearly rose at his.

That shows the atmosphere.

It is always there, subtly diffused through every Hindu and Mohammedan home. I was urging the Brahmin Sub-Registrar in Andapur to let his widowed sister-in-law come with some other young women to the Mission bungalow to be taught English. He professed to be anxious for women's education and discoursed freely on his regard for humanity, admitting that there was no real objection to departure from foolish customs, though he pronounced warningly—"The consensus of the whole community must be obtained first." All the time his wife was standing by, a thin, anæmic woman, looking tired; but neither she nor her sister could venture to sit down while the lord and master, himself seated comfortably on a string cot, held forth on the rights of humanity and his regard for them.

Comparisons are always odious, and may be very misleading, but I could not but be struck by the difference in the atmosphere of another Indian home I happened to visit a day or two after the Sub-Registrar's. It was the Christian apothecary's house at Dharmpalli. I was talking to husband and wife, both sitting down, about the near future when another little one is expected.

"Would you like a little boy or a little girl best?" I asked.

"I want another son," said the father, "but perhaps my wife would like a girl this time, I don't know."

She looked up at him quickly and laughed, then gave his knee a playful push, as if to say, 'You do know, quite well!'

A trifle—but without significance? Playful affection and happy familiarity it has not been my lot to see in Hindu homes.

I have seen companionship, though only rarely. The *Sheristadar* at Andapur, of the *Moodliar* caste, is an enlightened and kindly man. I remember visiting his house for the first time. To pass from the hot street through a double gateway to an inner courtyard round which were cool, deep verandahs with living-rooms behind, was a pleasure by itself. There a woman of thought and experience of life greeted me. She was glad to speak of many things. One could see her husband discussed things with her. Four sons had blessed the marriage; the father saw into the future and understood the impossibility of employment for the innumerable youths going in for a purely literary education. "We want our sons to study agriculture." Later on I was at the wedding of their eldest son, who was marrying a delightful and gifted Indian girl, herself also the daughter of enlightened parents who had delayed her marriage till the age of eighteen and allowed her to perfect her artistic bent; she was a charming painter. That marriage also promised to be ideal; alas! after only two years the young husband died.

It always meant a pleasure to me to visit the happy home of the *Sheristadar* and to meet the sweet and grave woman who was its mistress. When she died her husband was inconsolable. "She was my friend, my stay," he mourned. He scorned the idea of remarriage: "Put a child in Her place?"

But there are others who awaken less sympathetic and admiring feelings.

It was cholera season; one of the frequent outbursts of this terrible epidemic was sweeping over the district. A messenger stood in my verandah: "The wife of the head master of the High School has been taken ill; have you any medicine?"

I thought it wiser to administer it myself, and cycled to the house. The husband was sitting on the *pial* outside. "Yes, you can go in," he said, but did not offer to accompany me. Inside I found the patient looking already like a corpse, with the terribly sunk-in look of cholera cases, and the upper lip drawn away from the teeth. Flies were settling on her face. There was still life in her, for she lifted a feeble hand to brush them away. I went outside again.

"Is there no one here?" I asked the head master.

He gave a call and a servant woman came from the kitchen. She shook her head when I asked about boiled water and preparing invalid food. "She is dying."

It certainly was a hopeless case and a desolate deathbed, with no one near but a woman of alien race who could do nothing to help the dying woman except keep the flies off the poor face.

Afterwards I heard that when she was taken ill in the early morning the husband went out and immediately made funeral arrangements, then sat on his *pial* and waited for the end. Within two months he was married again.

Apart from such shocking callousness the ordinary atmosphere women live in is one of cramping limitations, where initiative of any sort is a crime.

"You do not know, we must do nothing without permission. We have to ask; if They do not like it we cannot come," is the perpetual answer to an urgent pressing to return my visit, or any similar invitation.

Yet sometimes the tables are turned. There are down-trodden spirits among the men on occasions! I met Achamma of Bukkuru. The trouble that girl's marital relations have given to many people, myself amongst the number! At first naturally, perhaps too naturally, my sympathies were with her. The young wife complained of cruelty, "It is hell to live with him." She ran back to her father, a widower in Bukkuru.

But by degrees it leaked out that much of the trouble was due in the first instance to the selfishness of the father, who had lusted after the seventy rupees marriage gift paid for his daughter, yet did not want to part with her services, and at the first hint of disagreement urged her to come back. Achamma has been a very naughty girl herself; there are rumours about a young Mohammedan. It is the husband who is patient and forgiving and asked her to return to his house. She refused; he then left his home and joined his wife in hers, —possibly with the generous desire to protect her good name. But he met with little gratitude. Though he earned the wages on which the whole household subsisted his wife hardly gave him enough rice to allay hunger, while an ample meal and titbits were set before the father. Half starved, the husband had to leave the house again and go back to his own.

As time went on and he found the situation intolerable he appealed to the elders of his caste. Backed by the whole strength of the caste, who threatened to excommunicate Achamma and her father if she still refused to come, he persuaded her to return home with him. But she came in no good mood. Arrived at the house she lay down and refused to stir. She would do no work, nor speak, nor anything but lie down and preserve an obstinate silence. The old mother-in-law did the cooking and all other housework, and tried to coax her into a better humour. In vain.

Watching her opportunity, Achamma ran back to Bukkuru and hid. The husband immediately followed and sought her in her father's house. She was not to be found. After some days she was discovered in the house of *Boyer* people. If a *Balji* woman goes and stays with *Boyers* her caste is lost, her honour doubtful. A great scene ensued. The husband was roused at last. Achamma's temper flared sky high. She tore off her *tali*[1] and threw it on the ground. Others watched aghast. If the husband took it it would indicate his final decision not to have her back. He picked it up and departed. Her affront to him in throwing down the *tali* in public was unforgivable.

The girl is now with her father, both are cast out by the caste, no fire, no water, no washing of clothes for either of them. There are occasions when caste rules act justly, if sternly.

Hindu marriages cannot be dissolved, since they are a religious and not a civil ceremony; so in Hinduism, unlike Mohammedanism, there is no divorce. The man may marry a second or third wife if he pleases, even in normal cases. In this particular instance it is a just provision, certainly, for none of the miserable upset is due to him. For Achamma, of course, respectability is finished. With her, a little more of the spirit ascribed by Sister Nivedita to all Hindu women would have been much to the good!

Her story shows that human nature is as variable in India as anywhere else, and confirms the dictum at the beginning of the chapter that generalizations are always risky.

And yet, is that in its turn an unsafe generalization? In spite of many exceptions, of women honoured, beloved, wise, or self-willed and rebellious and seeking for independence (which is not to be had), ought one not to acknowledge that the position of women in India must be radically altered before India can come to her own? Periodicals standing for

[1] Metal marriage-token.

reform bring forward from time to time horrible marital tragedies. From the comparatively few that come to light one may imagine the countless many that remain hidden. Hospitals for women can add their sad quota to the tale of suffering. The framework of custom regarding early marriage, wifely subjection, the general chatteldom of women, is such that it paves the way for tragedies in the hands of men inclined to be selfish or tyrannical. Many, of course, are kind and good-natured and better than their creeds. But even on such what must be the moral effect of being treated as a god, or, anyhow, as a superior and infallible being? Few of us are so safely ensconced in self-knowledge, and in the humility necessary for gaining that treasure, as to be able to stand a perpetual atmosphere of adulation without great risk.

Much is heard, and rightly, and indeed, not enough, of the tragedies of Indian women, their sufferings, their cries, and secret tears. What about the tragedies of Indian men, of the harm done to their souls, of inner avenues blocked and development towards free manhood retarded, by quite wrong conceptions about themselves, born of their treatment of women and of women's treatment of them? Broadly speaking (for the few thousand of well-educated women in India cannot yet be counted as an offset to, roughly, 160 millions of uneducated ones), independence, equality, have been denied to women. And is not the deplorable result the lack of inner independence of spirit in Indian men? Why are they so suspicious and easily resentful? Is it because in the most intimate part of their lives criticism can never come near them? Accustomed by their womenkind to a quite false position of godlikeness in the home there results a habit of taking themselves far too seriously, an inability to give and take which augurs ill for the future. For in the end it is only he who allows freedom to those about him who develops the inner capacity of taking the position of a free man to the outside world.

Every tyranny bears the seeds of punishment within itself, and this seems doubly the case when the oppressed are women. They seem to have this uncanny power. Treat them wrongly, deprive them of their dues anywhere—and the community or nation thus wronging them will be stamped with that identical weakness which was forced on their women.

For your own sake, for the world's sake, one wants to cry to India, Learn to treat your women rightly! Are not the times more than ripe for Indian men to set their house in order in this respect? They are educated enough (I am thinking of modern sciences like psychology), as they have always been intelligent enough, to understand that they are corrupting the source of their own manhood and actually poisoning the springs of their own virility by the denial of domestic freedom to their womenkind. Until this is granted the political freedom showing over the horizon is a mere sham.

The longed-for change cannot be brought about without pain and travail. The consciousness engendered by centuries of being considered a superior being, beyond criticism, will not be dislodged without desperate pain and discomfort. But until that narrow and difficult path is entered by India as a whole, her inner development is retarded, her progress towards true manhood blocked.

At present it is still blocked. The cry of oppressed womanhood still goes up. And another cry goes up, not perhaps so generally recognized. The sufferers are not only wives and widows, but parents. Fathers, as well as mothers.

I entered an Indian optician's shop in an Indian city, my mind on nothing but business connected with my glasses. But the Brahmin optician's mind was evidently elsewhere.

"Are you in trouble?" I asked at last.

"Oh madam, my trouble is greater than I can bear. My daughter, my eldest daughter! Two days ago we had the telegram that she was found in the well. Why could she not tell us she was unhappy? Oh those people! Again and again we asked that she should pay us a visit. There was always some excuse. She wrote once or twice that she wished to come. Why did I not go and see her? Her mother wished to go; but of course you cannot, unless they invite. What did they do to my daughter? Such a beautiful, gentle girl. What was her life? What made her do it? There is fire in my heart, I cannot bear it."

And what had been the fire in that girl's heart that she could not bear it and resolutely made an end?

At the time of writing these pages, a letter has come to an English friend from another distracted Indian father with whom there has been correspondence over his own unhappily married daughter. The husband seems to be verging on insanity in his outbreaks of cruelty. The father was urged not to let the girl return to such a home. But neither he nor the daughter are of the independent ones of the earth, and when the husband demanded it the wife returned. The father, after expressing his anxiety and grief, makes his excuse, as follows, to the Western reproach that he ought to have kept his daughter away from such misery and fear.

"Kindly do not forget," he writes, "that all Hindus believe in the superiority of the husband to his wife, and that a husband can do anything and everything to his wife. They even believe that the wife will go to heaven if she bears all kinds of treatment patiently and without complaint. Every husband, however highly he is educated and cultured, believes in this and at times may do most cruel things against his helpless wife. Forgive me if I say that many of your own Indian friends do not agree with you that love and justice should be shown to a woman, i.e. wife. But I myself agree. . . It is difficult for a woman in India to have justice. Neither the parents, nor the people on the side of the husband, nor the neighbours, can help a helpless woman. This is why thousands of ladies, even in great families, take refuge in *Ganga*, the water of wells, river or sea, and die a sad and fearful death every day in India. Tears fill my eyes as the heart feels it. What can a poor woman do when she has no refuge but must seek protection in death which she thinks better than lifelong unjust suffering? How long can women go on suffering like this?

"I believe if Hindus understood the spirit of the Lord Jesus they would become meek and lowly of heart. I know not what to say or think. India must go on suffering until their hearts turn to Jesus."

Do we know any other, or better, solution than this Indian sees for his country?

Education will do much. But what, in the first instance, was the force which started female education in India? Nothing within Hinduism or Mohammedanism or the British Government. It was Christian Missions which inspired this new thing which from small beginnings has grown till now we have university education, under various auspices.

The colleges for women which India possesses have not only given girlhood to the fortunate few thousand passing through them, but—in proving women's mental capacities, and causing an enlargement of their horizon—have opened the way for that happy intercourse and companionship between the sexes which is still far too rare in this country. Desperately are more women leaders wanted who can fight the battle of the weak and timid in the large-hearted and efficient way that some noble Indian women are doing at this moment, and it is to women's colleges that we must look to produce them. All power and success to them!

But unless we are to stand again before a disintegrating cleavage the extension of university education for women ought to mean more secondary education and that in its turn a greatly broadened basis of primary education. And here we are confronted by problems for some of which the solution seen by the Indian father seems the only one.

Anyone who contemplates grappling with the gigantic task of extending primary female education to the villages is staggered by the difficulties in the way. Girls must be taught by women. Where are the teachers to come from? In comparison with this social or domestic problem the further one of finance is a relatively small one. But, again, how are we to inspire the desire for the education of their daughters in the minds of peasant people to a degree sufficient to induce them to send these daughters to school? Even many educated people are still indifferent in this respect, as is shown by the very sparsely attended classes in some South Indian towns where high schools for girls have been opened, though the towns are the headquarter stations of districts. Then, suppose one had the teachers, what will fill them with the spirit of devotion and sacrifice necessary for such pioneer educational work in the villages? For the most backward need a high degree of culture and goodwill in those that make the attempt to raise them; yet too often, though not invariably, it has been found that highly trained Indians prefer work in conditions of culture matching their own. And indeed, how are conditions to be brought about which will enable women—say widows of whom so many thousands are living useless lives now, trained as teachers—to live safely and respectably in Indian villages? The bachelor woman, living away from her family and honourably earning a livelihood is a phenomenon that presupposes a change in social conditions at present still difficult to conceive.

For, still, there is against it the exaggerated sex-consciousness prevalent throughout the country. In spite of vehement denials it is still true to-day that among the bulk of the people women suggest sex and nothing else, intercourse with them apart from sex is not believed possible, hence there is no such thing as social intercourse between men and women. It would be an insult for a man to inquire after another man's wife, or to mention her at all directly. Let me give an example.

A Brahmin lawyer, a Member of the Legislative Council of our province, entered the railway compartment in which I was travelling. We had met before. That day he was in the humour to air grievances. At the time of the Moplah rebellion the Government contemplated sending a batch of Moplah prisoners to the town where my friend lived. The Chief Magistrate, a Britisher, deeply concerned with the welfare of his district, felt the responsibility of the presence of these prisoners to be a heavy one. According to my informant, the Collector voiced his fears when the Indian called on him.

"Suppose they break out? What about the women in the station? What about your wife, Mr. Kurupu Sami Iyer?" he was reported to have said. The mere memory made my fellow-traveller grow dark with rage.

"Yes, he had the effrontery to mention my wife to me! I wanted to reply, Yes, and what about Mrs. X?"

He meant he would have liked to hit back and return the affront by mentioning the Collector's wife.

"He would only have thought it polite of you to think of her safety, if you had," I assured my Indian friend.

But I combated that atmosphere in vain. He could not believe it would not have been taken, understood even, as rudeness.

Worse has happened to me. In an Indian family I was visiting with Dorcas the women were keen on asking questions about the English and their habits. My spinsterhood astonished them—this was usual; new to me, then, was their amazement at the fact of social dinners between all the white people in the station, the missionary included.

"But may you go to anybody?" I was asked next.

Naturally I thought the question referred to our ordinary social intercourse, and answered blithely in the affirmative.

I noticed Dorcas squirming. Then she spoke straight out. "Our Missiamma does not understand your meaning."

Imagine my horror when their real meaning was explained to me!

It must have been unusual: it never happened again; perhaps they were but recently moved from a village. One could not blame them; they never imagined any other sort of contact between men and women; if you were friendly it meant sex relationships.

Education, in favoured circles, is altering much; but even if it were possible to extend it within measurable time to the whole of India will it suffice to dissolve the fog of misunderstanding of the true nature of woman which rests on this land?

Long and steep is the road India has to climb before she reaches the height attained long ago by another Asiatic when he pronounced for all time: "There is neither bond nor free, neither male nor female, all are one in Christ Jesus."

The West learned, and is still learning, this lesson from Paul of Tarsus who, in his turn, sat at the feet of a Greater than he, also born in Asia. And in the passionate search for deliverance from sex-consciousness and the ceaseless desire for reform actuating pioneer spirits among India's own sons and daughters, will they not find in the divine *Guru* of Galilee and Golgotha the Way?

CHAPTER V

PRESSURE

OUR Indian Collector came round this morning. "Have you that statement ready about the Girls' High School for Andapur? The Director of Public Instruction will be here for the College function to-morrow. You will be there?"

"I will try and send over the statement to-day," I promised. "But about to-morrow—I am sorry, I fear I cannot. . . ."

"Your presence is particularly desired," he said firmly. I understood he wanted another woman to support his wife, who would feel awkward alone. (For just now, our officials in Andapur are all Indians—except one English bachelor.) Also he had his eye on my crotons for the festive occasion. "I will send over a cart for some pots."

I left other things and set to on the statement; afterwards glanced dismally at my wardrobe, very much the country cousin's, and started overhauling a frock. The post was brought in. A fellow-missionary arriving to-day! Laws of hospitality demand cakes. They are not the cook's *forte*, so I set to and made some. The cook burnt one and left the other in the back verandah where a squirrel ate half. So now hastily to make more! The last butter-tin in the storeroom was opened and turned out to be rancid. What a life.

My real mind nowadays is on building; for the new bungalow is going up. I pore over building-books at night, frantically striving to increase my knowledge. The subject pursues me into my dreams. I had been reading that walls should be sized. What exactly was size? Didn't we have it in bathrooms at home? Last night I dreamed I entered a bungalow; a woman there had a barrel full of whitewash and brought a white lump of sorts to drop in. "Stop, stop!" I shrieked. "What is that? Is it size? Let me look at it!"

But she only gave me a supercilious glance and turned away. By the time I had reached the barrel the lump had plopped hopelessly to the bottom. My rage at the lost opportunity was so great that I woke up.

A new puzzle, besides ever fresh revelations of my ignorance, is confronting me now. For the moment I can see no solution. The bungalow where I am now will be wanted in two months for other tenants. This is an old and fixed arrangement. The new and permanent house cannot be finished for another eight or ten months. To tide me over the interval I had secured a small bungalow. Or I thought I had. But the contract was only a verbal one; and now the faithless owner had suddenly a better offer and has let the place as a Government office. There is not another house to be had in Andapur. Does "our daily bread" include "our daily roof"?

I am not the only female in creation with housing and building troubles. In the pomegranate-bush by the verandah of the present house a pair of bulbuls are building. Their goings-on are instructive. The little cock never does a stroke of work, not one. But he sees that his wife does! She flies about looking for grass and straw, comes back with some and dives into the bush. *He* comes back with nothing, but sits empty-clawed on the rain-tree near by. If she is rather long inside the bush he gets impatient and twitters crossly: "Make haste, oh feminine slowcoach!" When at length she flies out and dashes for more straw, he is after her with a loud shout that says plainly, "I'll see you don't flirt with other birds!" She comes back with another straw; he, as usual, with none, only sits over her in the rain-tree and lectures her. But once she had the laugh of him. Lecturing is no doubt exhausting work; he must have got drowsy; anyhow I saw her fly out of the bush without being observed by him. Presently he came to from his nap and screamed, "Are you not coming *yet*?" But no humble little chirp from the bush answered.

Surprised, he slipped inside. Empty! The screech of rage with which he dashed off proclaimed his entire loss of equilibrium, and I felt pleased to see him suffer. Now there are two eggs; hopefully I waited for a third, for the school museum—but no more forthcame. If only the lazy old cock had the trouble of laying and hatching them I would take them several times over, merely to teach him a lesson; but though birds are not supposed to be able to count, I cannot really believe that; out of two they would surely miss one, and then he would scold her beyond bearing. Never marry a bulbul.

My building troubles were nearly as great as Mrs. Bulbul's. A way out of my dilemma for a residence had occurred to me at last. It was to build a room on to the maistry's room already existing on the new compound, and use these two, one as bedroom, the other as study-dining-office-room. The consent had to be asked of our Local Committee. Local Committee had no rule and no precedent to meet the emergency. In the end they decreed a monthly rent allowance till the bungalow is finished, which is a proper groove and procedure. It will not pay for the little house—but, never mind, here goes. Precious weeks have already been lost. We dug the foundations. Rain, rain, rain. This, since it washed away the cholera which had been abroad in the town, also took away the builders' excuse for bolting on that score, and so far served me well; but the water filled the trenches to the brim; we could not build foundations in the water, the softened sides began to cave in; days of delay occurred and the builders grew restive again. Then the rain stopped for a while; but news came that the maistry's wife had fallen ill; he had to go off to the other end of nowhere to bring her home. During his absence I had to act for him, and hoped for his speedy return; but the heavens spurted forth again; rivers rose to flood level, railway bridges broke down, or became too endangered for traffic; the days passed without the longed-for arrival. Meanwhile foundations had been put in; walls began to rise; timber for door and window frames was wanted. When the maistry returned at last he was sent post-haste to Bangalore to buy the timber. He saw it loaded on the railway and it was to reach here in two days. Three days passed, four, five. I made wild inquiries. No answer. Timber had gone to Timbuktu, I surmised (no pun intended). Sure enough, on the tenth day came news that by mistake it had been sent to Gadag, past two big junctions beyond Andapur! The builders wanted to bolt again as the work was held up for these frames, which have to be built into the walls. I resolved to take the frames destined for the upper storey of the bungalow; they were a different size—that cannot be helped. The errant scantlings arrived at last—after seventeen days. When counted, sixteen roof rafters were missing; oh, thieving railway! What was to be done now? The roof must go on, as more rain threatened. I took the rafters destined for the bungalow back verandah, first-class timber, and charged the railway company for the difference as well as the loss. Will they pay compensation? The roof couples went on, the reepers were nailed, the tiles followed. Then the tiles ran short by about two hundred and fifty or so. But in the D.P.W. Compound I had seen surplus stock of tiles lying round; I asked the Overseer to let me have two hundred and fifty. "All right, take them." I took them. They turned out to be the wrong size. The reepers had to be taken off and fixed again to suit the new tiles. When they had been put on the Engineer visited the place, in a bad humour. The Overseer had sold surplus stock to me before; he and I thought it was all right; but the Engineer would listen to nothing, only sent *chits*, "Sorry, but the tiles must be returned." I returned them, anathematized him for being the limit and wired to Bangalore for more tiles.

Meanwhile in the maistry's room, adjacent to which this building was going on, a baby had been born. It died after two days. The maistry, an affectionate man, was distracted and full of grief. The workmen struck work and sat and grieved with him out of respect. Then news came that plague had broken out in their native village and two builders bolted. Further rain fell here, so no local coolies would come, as everyone was off to field-work. The poor wife lay dying in the little room; no work could be carried on. In the end she died. The maistry went off to mourn. I was left with a few workmen and the days of grace running short.

The door in the wall between the old room and the new had yet to be knocked in, the roof of their kitchen, which is to be my bathroom, raised—as it was then I could not stand upright in it; the whole place to be plastered and white-washed. I drove ahead.

Then the workmen came and said, "No lime." I went from pillar to post to get it, but no one had any. In this rainy weather it cannot be procured fresh. At last I heard of some in the possession of a temple, stored for repairs. The temple authorities were hunted out; from one Brahmin to another I was sent, behaving my politest to each—and in the end got my lime. Only four days left now to finish. As it was market-day no carts were available; and the next day it poured again—not for years have we had so violent a monsoon!—so it could not be ground. But midday showed signs of clearing up; we started grinding—and mixed and plastered the moment it was ground. A neck-to-neck race it remained to the end; but, impossible as it had seemed, the little house was finished—on the last day before I had to leave the old bungalow. It was built in a month.

Not for a moment do I believe that human resourcefulness accomplished this. It is, surely, the response of the Invisible. Matters committed to that Kingdom seem to bring into play incalculable potencies which make them come out right in the end, however wrong they seem to be going all along. How trite it sounds! What a fight they nevertheless represent, these inner acts of faith!

And then come further thoughts.

Is not our idea of God rather limited? Philosophy, emotion, we easily connect with Him; poetry, music, yes;—but building?

He built this cottage, that is all I know.

No, I do not mean anything repellently anthropomorphic. I mean what Paget means when he calls the Kingdom of God "that invasion and conquest and transfiguration of this present life by the powers of the life to come." (By the way, that is the best definition of the term "Kingdom of God" that I know.) Anything will serve for such an invasion: bricks and refractory builders, unhelpful engineers, adverse weather, thieving railways,—all the circumstances that for us here and now make up "this present life." Conquered, transfigured, by the powers of the life to come; how glorious then may be our ordinary human life anywhere!

CHAPTER VI

THE GREAT ROCK

OUR district is the smallest in the province; even so it is about as big as Yorkshire. But in population it does not reach three-quarters of a million, being dry and arid and stony. We have no cities to boast about; our largest towns—even the headquarter station I live in—have no more than ten thousand inhabitants, and of towns of this size there are scarcely half a dozen; the rest of us live in villages.

The town second in importance in this district is Penukonda. It is described (inaccurately, as events turned out) in an old inscription as "a god-built city, the surrounding fortifications of which no man could boast of conquering." [1] Here, over three hundred years ago, the last kings of the now forgotten Hindu empire of Vijayanagar made a stand against Mohammedan invaders. Venkatapa Deva Raja of Penukonda inflicted a crushing defeat on Mohamed Shah of Golkonda on the banks of the Penair river. But he could not stay the oncoming hordes, who eventually swept through the pass, stormed the great fortress rock of Penukonda and fell upon the temples and shrines dotted about on it; the gods and goddesses were wrenched from their niches and pedestals and thrown down the hill by the idol-hating Moslems. To this day the traces of their destructiveness remain. On my walk from the station I came across defaced and broken stone images lying about in ditches—they are to be had for the picking up, but their weight ensures their being left where they are.

The Mohammedan conquerors passed in their turn. Old victors and vanquished now live side by side under the British raj. To-day Penukonda consists of two parts: the fort where Hindus live, chiefly Brahmins; and Babai Pet,

[1] Quoted from a Telugu brochure, *Venkata II*, by T. Siva Sankaram.

inhabited by Mohammedans, of the poorer kind mostly—also the haunt of innumerable beggars of both religions. Over both parts towers the great fortress rock, the remnants of towers and royal residences still crowning its summit. English officials residing in the district, and attracted by the coolness up there, have at times spent parts of the hot weather in those forsaken halls; till coolies, weary of the daily ascent with provisions, burnt the thatched roofs covering them. Now only a tower or two is left, which the hill monkeys consider to be their exclusive abode, as unwary visitors, spending a night there, discover to their cost. Before my startled eyes a long hairy paw suddenly was stretched through one of the narrow slits in the thick wall that do duty for windows, and in a twink drew out my toothbrush, left unsuspectingly on the sill.

In the town below life flows on as it did in days of old. Temples and shrines on the hill may be denuded and old fortifications have gone, but the rock of Hinduism is as strongly fortified in human hearts as in the past. The old cry, "Rock, Rock! when wilt thou open?" uttered by a fervent soul before an inaccessible China, might still be echoed in India. Or so I thought, when I wended my way one morning to the town. The entrance lies through several massive gateways. In a deep recess of the main gate stands a huge image of *Hanuman*, the monkey god, about ten feet high, painted all over in brilliant colours. Coming upon it suddenly, I was startled by the towering shape. What kind of suggestion, I wondered, would it convey to children as they passed and glanced fearfully into the darkness?

Some women, rickly dressed in silk *saris* and decked with jewels, approached and beckoned to the priest. He came forward and they handed him a coconut. He accepted the offering and lit the lamp they held out to him at the sacred flame before the shrine, spilling some oil on the floor, where it burned on. Then he broke the coconut, handing one half back to the worshippers and distributing the other to some boys hovering near. One of the women meanwhile bowed towards the Image, clasping her hands and lifting them, palm pressed to palm, once or twice in supplication; her lips moved as her hands were raised. For the fraction of a moment she stood rapt—then her worship, which had occupied less than a minute, was over. The whole performance of offering and breaking the coconut, of lighting lamps and saying a prayer, was finished in about three minutes. Then the women passed on, chatting to one another and taking no notice of me standing silently by. A Brahmin widow came, and I witnessed a repetition of the little scene, save that her prayer took longer.

When she, too, had gone I drew nearer to the shrine and tried to think their thoughts after them. Though I have travelled far from my former feelings about Hindu temples it was not easy. I remembered the first such visit, soon after arriving in India. Whom did they worship, since it was not the God revealed in the Bible? Did they serve devils here, I had then thought fearfully. So foolish was I and ignorant. I have learnt better now. May the exaggerated shapes of these images and idols—many arms and legs in some cases, and other members too in great plurality—not be the attempt to express a faith in more than human powerfulness and fruitfulness; as well as the bewilderment caused by India's many catastrophic occurrences, drought, floods, pestilences, famines, etc., occasioned by who knows what arbitrary and enormous powers? Grotesque as they are, the images, surely, express searchings after God? Is there not a true and permanent element in the human effort to visualize Him? Has it not persisted through centuries of Christianity?

"Some folk as can afford,
So I've heard say,
Set up a sort of cross
Right in the garden way,
To mind them of the Lord."

And when it is carried further and the Divine thought and presence are recognized in His creation have we not reached its explanation?—or should I say, sublimation?

"But I, when I do see
Thik apple tree
And stoopin' limb
All spread with moss,
I think of Him
And how He talks with me."

• • • • • •

And when I die pray God I see
At very last thik apple tree
And stoopin' limb,
And think of Him,
And all He been to me." [1]

One Man stated authoritatively that God had responded to the human cry to see Him, in the Incarnation.

Then that also which prompted the worship I had just witnessed was an indication of man's eternal longing to find God. As best they could the women were feeling after Him.

Yet how terribly misleading, how stultifying to these very desires of their spirits, is such worship. Was this a place to take off one's shoes? I gazed again upon the object towards which the soul activates of the women had been directed. Of fantastic shape and overawing size, painted threateningly in carmine and ochre, greasy with the oil of innumerable offerings, the monkey god gleamed grimly and terrifyingly from the darkness of the recess. Could it convey a single right idea of God? It could very easily inspire terror, certainly. No wonder there are many indications in the religious life of the people to show they want their gods farther away. *Hanuman* would be no refuge in time of trouble. Indeed, if he were inclined to be active it would certainly be wise to propitiate him. Was this what the women's devotion signified? "We give you this, accept it, leave us alone and in

[1] A. Bunston, *Under a Wiltshire Apple Tree.*

peace,"—is not this what such crude animistic worship frequently denotes?

Are *Hanuman* and his fellow-gods responsible for the fear-complex which holds India in thrall, and for the inability I have met so often, to believe in the goodwill of God, with its further disastrous consequence of inability to believe in the goodwill of man, manifested so glaringly in modern times?

These reflections came afterwards; on that morning I was watching facts.

Farther on in the bazar, where the street of private houses forked away from that of the shops, stood a great banyan-tree. On the platform built round its base, snake idols, carved in stone, leaned against the trunk. A high-school student, with his books under his arm, stepped on to the platform, laid down his books and prostrated himself before the stones; rose and sank down again, till he had measured his length all round the tree by six or seven prostrations. I watched in fascination. No one else took the least notice; it was a customary sight. The youth stood in silent prayer for another moment, then gravely picked up his books and went on. What had been his thought? To ask the divine blessing on his work that day—perhaps specially needed for an examination? Or was it just to gain merit? Or was perchance his young heart already unwisely burdened by domestic cares? The girls' side in the woes of early marriage is naturally most to the fore in my experience, but a great deal might also be said about the young men's. There, too, tragedies occur; failures, breakdowns, suicides, because the mental strain of studies and examinations, concurring with the emotional strain of domestic difficulties—the demands of "in-laws," illness of a young wife, birth or death of a child—proves too heavy a weight for shoulders so young. What help had this student petitioner been seeking by his earnest prostrations near the public street?

But I had private visits to pay and passed on to the house of some Brahmin friends. Scarcely had I greeted the inmates and been invited to sit down when a man came in who seated himself on the floor, cleared his throat and looked expectantly at the ladies of the house.

"He is the newspaper," said my hostess.

"Oh, he is the newspaper," I repeated blankly.

Then I noticed the new arrival wore a coat with a device on either shoulder, "Walking News" on one side, "News Coat" on the other

It was explained to me that he collected news wherever he could, local and other, wrote them in a note-book and went round houses of clients in the mornings to read them. For Indian ladies who cannot read, a welcome boon.

The newspaper having made its appearance began its tale. We listened with respect to the announcement that the Viceroy's lady was ill, that plague had broken out in the district, that certain events had taken place in an eastern war, that Miss C., the missionary from Andapur, had arrived in the town. There was nothing in voice or classification to distinguish the degree of historic importance of the items.

In the next Brahmin family visited a baby had been born. All night in her agony the young mother—who was only fourteen!—had been calling out for her English friend. A visit was permitted. The usual horrors were somewhat mitigated. Though the window was tightly shut and the small room hot and airless it was not rendered intolerably stifling by the customary fire, burned to keep away demons; a small lamp was all the concession made to this superstition. No one took the trouble to show me the baby, as it was "only a girl."

The young mother lay there listless, worn out and deeply disappointed probably, at not having a son. Yet the baby was a nice, well-formed child. I dared not, however, say much on that score, as that might bring ill-luck and would therefore be considered unfriendly. But another inquiry might be made. "Has the mother had food?"

"Not yet."

"But she is exhausted."

"They are getting it ready."

At that, or rather at strongly-worded advice, it had to be left; in matters of food it would be an insult to suggest any practical interference. Sacred are the rules of caste.

Also difficult for us Westerners to learn. Going back to the front room a delightful baby of about ten months was laughing and crowing in her mother's arms.

"Will she come to me?" I asked, holding out my arms eagerly.

In embarrassed haste the mother stripped off the baby's little jacket and held out the naked infant to me.

I remembered the trouble I had inadvertently caused in another Brahmin home by touching a baby wearing a little coat. A servant had to be called, who took off the defiled garment and then clumsily inserted the howling child into another jacket, the mother standing in front, scolding and giving instructions, but not offering to help as it would have "defiled" her.

But a baby with no clothes on at all was apparently beyond possibility of defilement by the white stranger.

Is not the body more than the raiment? one wants to ask. But logic is not a thing you must ask for in India.

On the way home I went into the post-office on business. A new Postmaster presided over the establishment. I could not help staring at him. For it seemed to me he had the face of the young man whom Christ looked upon and loved.

"Yes, I have only lately come," he answered my inquiry. "I am a Christian. May I come and see you, and will you visit my mother?"

In the evening, sitting in his house after office hours, I

listened to his amazing story, which I wrote down immediately and give now in his own words.

"From childhood up I have been zealous in the Hindu religion. With my whole heart I worshipped two special sages, always hoping they would be mediators on the way to the supreme Being. I was not educated in a Mission school, I never heard of Christ. But when I was about fourteen a friend who had been to a Mission school showed me a little tattered English Bible. I asked if this were the Christian book, for by then I had heard of them, and said I should like to read it.

"I opened it in the middle and began with the Psalms. I found them wonderful, describing exactly our own experiences and full of the purest worship of God. But there was nothing in them about Christ, which surprised me. I read and re-read them, all the time worshipping our own gods with great devotion. I turned to other parts of the Bible, but I could not understand them, and I kept on wondering why they too did not mention Christ.

"Then I was told of an old evangelist in our neighbourhood. I went to him and told him how beautiful I had found the Psalms; but why did they not speak of Christ? Who was He? I had always understood Christians worshipped Him.

"The evangelist showed me the gospels and advised me to study them. I went home and directly I had leisure in the evening started reading them. As I read His story such a love for the wonderful Christ sprang up in my heart that I forgot all else. I read till midnight, unconscious of time. My mother came in and scolded me for being so late; whatever was I reading all that time, she asked suspiciously. Many an evening after that I read the New Testament half the night.

"Up till then I had been zealously worshipping at all the temples and performed all religious ceremonies. But now I began to think if Christ were the true Saviour all this was not necessary. When this thought had once become clear to me I left off all worship of Hindu gods, suddenly. My friends and relations were astonished.

" 'What is the matter with you?' they asked, when I would no longer come with them to temples and ceremonies. They became suspicious, especially when they heard that I had begun to associate with Christians. They questioned me, saying they had heard these rumours against me. I evaded a direct reply, merely saying I was as religious as ever. But they were not satisfied.

"Then a domestic ceremony was to be held in my house. I invited my friends. Not one of them came.

" 'I will ask my new friends,' I thought, and invited Christians. They came and I made a feast for them, though I did not sit down to eat with them.

"The news spread in the town. People ran to tell my old mother that I was forsaking caste and joining the Christians.

"She came running to me. When she saw me she fell down and clasped my feet.

" 'My son, my son,' she cried, 'do not break my heart! Do not leave the old ways and bring shame upon us all!'

" 'Please rise, Mother,' I said uncomfortably. I could not bear her to hold my feet. 'Please rise. I promise you I will do nothing to bring shame upon you.'

" 'I will not rise till you promise me that you will never join the Christian way!' she cried. 'I will lie here and hold your feet till you give me that promise.'

"I could not move, I could not treat my mother roughly—but how could I promise what she wished? Christ had my heart. Yet all religions hold sacred the duty to parents. I stood there in an agony of conflict. What was I to do?

"When she saw me hesitate my mother wept in anguish. 'Give me this promise, son, or I lie here all night and tomorrow there is the well for me.'

" 'Help me, God,' I prayed. 'Show me what to do. It cannot be Thy will I should break my mother's heart. Nor will

I forsake Jesus Christ. What shall I do? What shall I say to her?'

"My mind was pierced with sorrow. A great darkness was round me. I went on praying in my heart. Suddenly a great peace fell. I knew what to say.

"'Rise, mother. I promise you I will not join the Christian way until you agree to it,' I told her. 'I will not leave you, I will do nothing secretly, but I will pray that God will move your heart to like this religion also. I will wait for your free consent.'

"Then she rose, comforted. That consent she was sure she would never give.

"But from that time on I tried to teach her in every possible way. I asked the Bible-woman to visit her and give her instruction. My mother is a deeply religious woman and liked her stories and lessons.

"Once we went to Tirupati. I took my mother round the temples and shrines and showed her the darker side of Hindu worship and how much evil is connected with temples. Then we went inside, as my mother wished to break a coconut to the god.

"But the priest sat before the shrine and said we must pay him four annas for breaking it and another four annas for sprinkling camphor.

"We had left the house without taking money with us.

"'Sir,' I said to the priest, 'I am sorry. We are not prepared. We have no money with us. Please break the coconut, so that my mother may feel she has performed her devotion.'

"'I will not,' he said rudely. 'Bring your four annas.'

"'My mother is very religious,' I urged. 'The money is a trifle to us; you shall have it later. Please do not hurt my mother by refusing to allow her to perform her act of worship.'

"But he got quite angry and threw our coconut away, nor would he let us enter the shrine.

"We went out, and I said to my mother, 'You see this is no spiritual worship. He cared not for your true feeling of devotion, only for his four annas.'

"My mother admitted it. That morning shook her faith in Hinduism. She had been a most zealous follower of it hitherto; she worshipped every image and neglected no ceremonies. But after that morning she became less diligent in these things and began to pray to Jesus Christ.

"My wife had been easy to teach. I instructed her myself. I taught her a short prayer and she prayed it daily. Every night I prayed with her.

"In the eighth month of my wife's pregnancy my mother became anxious. It is the custom of our people to perform at that time a ceremony of propitiation to a certain devil goddess. Unless something is sacrificed to her it is believed she will kill the child. It must be performed in the middle of the night; a sheep, or some fowls, are killed at her shrine. My mother was afraid. You do not know how deeply these old fears are rooted in us. At times I was afraid myself. Even to us educated people the world is full of malignant powers. But I steadily refused to give way. Jesus Christ alone is our Helper, I maintained; we will pray to Him and not to any demon goddess. I forbade my mother to perform any worship on our behalf at that shrine. She was terrified.

"'Surely the child will die!' she cried fearfully.

"But I assured her that prayer to Christ would avail.

"When the time came near I would have no Hindu helper in the house. Word was sent to me at my office one day at five o'clock that my wife was ill. I prayed without ceasing while still at my work. I went home at seven o'clock, sat on the *pial* and prayed. A few minutes afterwards my mother came running out and said, 'The child is born.' I burst into tears of joy.

"My mother, according to our custom, wished to keep my wife without food for three days; but I said it was a foolish superstition and myself brought her bread and coffee. And she was well, and the child was well, and my mother's faith grew stronger.

"But though she said she would serve Jesus Christ she would not be baptized, nor allow me to be. I waited and prayed. I waited for her altogether about three years. Then I arranged for my baptism to take place in another town. When the day fixed for it dawned I told my mother. I said, 'How is your mind? Do you think more of salvation, or of all these people?'

" 'Of salvation,' she answered.

" 'Then follow me to church,' I said. 'The cart will be here in half an hour.'

"When it arrived she was ready. My mother and my wife and I were all received together. It was like a miracle.

"Great trouble followed. My caste fellows nearly poisoned me. I had to leave my own country, I was not safe. I obtained this transfer here.

"My mother still needs instruction. A fortnight ago my child had some kind of eruption. She wanted to call in the enchanters. I said, No, let us pray in the name of Christ. The child shall be well or ill, according to the will of God. Next morning the eruption was less and the third day quite gone.

"And now trouble is beginning in this town. The high-caste people are trying to convince me that what I have done is wrong. But oh, I know!

"It is not only in outward things like illness. I know that Christ changes one's disposition where it needs changing. Some time ago my mother and I had a disagreement. That had occurred before. Whenever it happened I held aloof and would not speak to her till she spoke to me. But now I had no peace of mind. I went and apologized to her first and said that was the Christian way."

While he was talking the old mother came and bustled round cheerfully; the young wife also appeared and proudly exhibited her firstborn. "Come to us to-morrow when he is at the office, then we will have a talk," both women said.

I had been listening lost in wonder. The great fortress rock of Hinduism, with its guarded gateways of caste customs and prejudices, its social evils, its crude idol worship and age-long fears, often seems wellnigh impregnable.

Yet Jesus Christ finds His way in.

CHAPTER VII

BY THE WAYSIDE

SHE was a very tired old woman. Every day the path through the fields to her village seemed longer. The Indian sun smote fiercely, she pulled her red *sari* over her shaven head. Other wayfarers passed her, coolie women going to their day's labour, chatting volubly; some with babies on their hips; nearly all with flowers in their hair; a tiny disc of shiny metal ornamenting their noses, bangles on their arms, and three or four necklaces round their brown throats. They gave her a wide berth. It was not very lucky to find a widow on their path. Neither party gave greeting to the other. For widow as the old woman might be she was a Brahmin; her plain red robe proclaimed it loudly. Coolies of low Sudra caste were infinitely beneath her notice. For them to come within touching distance would have been sin. They knew it, and passing round her hastened on their way.

Wearily she trudged on, carrying a large empty basket. The path crossed a road where it dipped into a stream-bed. Low parapets guarded the sides. It was a convenient resting place. She sat down and untying the corner of her *sari* extracted some betel-nut. With the aid of the small pestle and mortar slung on her girdle she pounded it into powder; then, after adding a tiny scrap of lime, rolled it up in a betel-leaf and sat contentedly chewing the mixture. It took away one's hunger to do that. Not that it mattered so much now, being hungry. In former years she had felt it more keenly, though the complete fast days coming twice a month helped to habituate her to its pangs. Hunger, in any case, was not so hard to bear. It was thirst that was so intolerable. Throughout the long hot days, on the walks in the burning sun to get the vegetables she sold—from sunrise to sunrise, never a drop must pass her lips. They cracked and blistered sometimes, the throat swelled till she could hardly swallow, not even when the prescribed fast was over and she might drink.

Ah well, it was her one hope of salvation, faithfully following these rules. "*Swami, Naraina!*" her lips murmured, as she sat leaning against the parapet. She might name the great Name, that was not forbidden even to a widow. Indeed, it was her chief way of gaining merit. Life was very lonely. Did God hear? Did He take any notice of her prayers? There was never any sign or answer. Yet one must go on serving, she knew, though without hope of reward. "*Swami, Naraina!*" she repeated, and looked dreamily down the road.

White and dusty it wound over the plain. Now, in the beginning of the hot weather, the banyan-trees lining it stood stark and bare. But in between them the delicate neem-trees swayed in their fresh robe of feathery green leaves, throwing shadows of fine tracery across the road. No cart or other traffic could be seen; the quiet country road was little used, except in the evenings, when *jatkas* raced along to take adventurous villagers to the distant station where mail trains halted for a few minutes.

But now a movement in the distance caught the old woman's eye. What could it be? It approached more swiftly than a man walking. Was it a rider? But no thud of horse's hoofs interrupted the drowsy silence, nor creak of wheels. Yet wheels there were, revolving fast, catching the glint of the sun, an immovable figure on them—a demon?

"*Swami, Naraina!*" muttered the Brahmin woman apprehensively.

The apparition had reached the farther bank of the stream. There was no water in it, only sand. The wheels rushed into it. The spectator could see now that feet were working the wheels—but something went wrong, in another moment feet, and whatever was on them, lay sprawling in the sand. She remembered now seeing a strange vehicle like this once before, a white man had come along the road one day on only wheels. So this was another of them. Was he killed? *Swami, Naraina!* let her hasten away before she was defiled by the sight of death; she, a pure Brahmin, to be thus contaminated when she had already worshipped and bathed to-day at sunrise, and had not another *sari* if this one were polluted!

But before her stiff limbs had risen her eyes reassured her. The figure in the sand had got up and was shaking the sand from its garments. Skirts! So it was a woman. Yes, evidently a woman; she was looking round the landscape with a vexed expression.

Memory stirred in the old widow. Thus, yes, thus had she felt on a day in the far past when she had followed in the wake of the home-coming cattle to collect their droppings for fuel to cook her modest meals. She had filled her basket and then suddenly slipped on a loose stone and fallen, the contents of the basket, still soft, had bespattered her garment. She had looked round with mortification to see if there were any witnesses. There were none. She remembered her relief, —and now, even so, did the white woman look round, her face cheerful seeing an empty road, with none to mark her discomfiture. She pulled up her machine in the stream-bed and pushed it towards the bank. Then her eyes fell upon the red-robed figure, shrinking against the parapet. The wayfarer stood still and the two women regarded each other.

"Why are you sitting all alone in this wilderness? asked the new-comer.

"I rest a little, on the way to my village," said the Brahmin. "There, beyond the hill over there, I have to go."

"Your home is there?" continued the white woman.

"I have no home. Some of our caste people let me sleep in their verandah and cook in a corner of their yard," said the widow.

The cyclist's gaze travelled over the red *sari*. "Your husband died some time ago?"

"Seventy years ago."

The other woman's eyes grew very pitiful. A child widow. Indeed, a widowed baby she must have been; being still able to walk from village to village selling vegetables she could hardly be above seventy herself. The long white road disappearing into the distance seemed like this woman's life, lonely and purposeless. But is there any road that leads nowhere?

"You have no people?" she asked again.

"All dead, all dead long ago," sighed the old woman. "I am quite alone."

"Not quite alone," said the other wayfarer.

"Quite alone," repeated the Indian widow.

"Not one of them is forgotten," murmured the other, "by the Father."

A slow light came into the deeply furrowed face. "Yes, *Swami*, *Naraina*," she responded; "I sit here in the wilderness and say '*Swami*, *Naraina*.'"

"God is your Companion?" asked the younger woman.

"I say *Swami*, *Naraina*; it is all I know," repeated the widow.

"What is your name?" questioned the other

"Hanumakka."

Hanuman, the monkey god, mused her listener. Named after him.

"Where are *your* people?" asked the Brahmin in her turn.

"Far away. I have none here. As you see, I travel alone."

"Where is your husband? How many children have you?"

"None. I was never married."

The Indian woman looked at her in surprise. "Never married?" Her gaze became more penetrating. Wonder crept into her eyes. "No husband, no children. Yet she does not look unhappy," she murmured. "And she is not old, as I am."

"No, not unhappy," confirmed the other. "Because of the great companionship, Hanumakka."

Her listener looked significantly at the solitary cycle, leaning against the parapet. "Who is with you?"

"He who came to reveal the Father to whom you pray so much. You also are remembered by Him. Not forgotten by Him are any of His children."

In the neem-tree near, a pair of wild pigeons cooed loudly. A gust of wind swirled up the sand in the stream-bed and drove it into their eyes.

"I must go now," said the old woman, taking up her basket.

"But not alone," said her new friend. "A great *Guru* long ago said that not even a sparrow was forgotten by God. And you are more than many sparrows."

"*Swami, Naraina*," said the widow patiently—"all the way, all the long way, I have said '*Swami, Naraina.*' Day by day. It may be as you say, that God is kind. We know not. I am old now, I cannot learn more."

Slowly she crossed the road to the field-path leading to the village beyond the hill.

The white woman wheeled her cycle forward. Before mounting, she gazed again after the retreating figure, hobbling painfully, in evident fatigue. She thought of the unwelcomed arrival, of the comfortless verandah and courtyard awaiting her.

"Ah, who shall know the dreary woe?"

she murmured. But—"*Swami, Naraina.*" Had no light ever come in response to the old widow's groping after the Divine, her daily "*Swami, Naraina*"? Surely these had come up before God as the prayers and alms of another seeker long ago?

. . . "and who the splendour see?
There's One who walked with starry feet the Eastern road by me."

"But she is so alone, she has no home even of her own." The traveller as she cycled on seemed still to remonstrate with someone.

> "Yet not unled, but shepherded, by One they cannot see,
> The One who walked with starry feet the Eastern road by me." [1]

[1] Evelyn Underhill, *The Uxbridge Road.* With apologies for substituting "Eastern" for "Western."

CHAPTER VIII

EMBER DAYS

A LETTER from home just received contains the sentence that it is always worth while to enter into other people's lives, that it brings its own reward. I am on the look-out for that reward just now, for this is an account of my last twelve hours.

The day began in Dharmpalli, where our Mission workers had come together for special meetings. After the final meeting Radha walked in.

"I have a word"—beginning to gulp. I knew what these gulps meant. Nobody loves me, is the gist.

"Joseph"—gulp—"Joseph says I am bad."

"Well, Radha, suppose he does. Does it matter very much?"

"Oh, oh, oh!"—the flood-gates yielded wide. "He says I am bad, and you say it does not matter very much. My sister is dead, and I have no one in the world!" The stream flowed on. Knowing it a relief I let it flow; but grief merged into anger.

"He says . . . he says . . . Ought he to say such things?"

"No. But that is his business and not ours. Our business, Radha—what is just now in your heart?"

"Anger," she said promptly, in her frank way.

"Yes, anger and bitterness. . . ." Here the Collector's *peon* marched in holding out a large official envelope. "The permit to go to Punneru is herewith cancelled." These terrible war restrictions—the long-looked-forward-to prospect of a little rest and fellowship with friends dashed from me in a moment. Inwardly I staggered a little; but there was no time to dwell on disappointment, for Radha still stood there, desiring to hear Joseph condemned. When she went at last, mollified, I hope, Rebekka the school teacher entered.

"I must speak to you. You have to leave now for the station? I will walk with you. It is about Dina the Bible-woman. She took great offence because last month you sent all the salaries to me. I sent a message to Dina that the money had come and I would bring it to her in the evening. But the schoolgirl gave the message wrong and said, 'The money has arrived, come and take it.' Dina was angry and said, 'Do I go to her to take the money?' When I went to give it to her she would not speak to me. Since then she hardly ever speaks to me. Also there is Rama Rao, the other teacher; he is always setting the children against me; now even the conductress won't obey me,"—here followed further long tales about the misdeeds of Rama Rao, all the way to the station and on the platform until the train moved out.

I should have remembered their sensitiveness; the one who distributes salaries is considered boss; one cannot eradicate the Indian notion that money lends dignity; my parsimony in sending a lump sum was ill-advised.

At Andapur Ruth awaited me. "You called David and you called Susan to the meetings at Dharmpalli, and you did not call me. For this I have much pain in my mind. And to-day Mr. Paul came to the school and marked the register. If I cannot be trusted to mark the register in the absence of the head master, what happiness is there for me in this work?"

"But, Ruth, I told everyone that adults only, no children, were allowed to attend the meetings. How could you have left your two little ones behind? And the only reason I asked Mr. Paul to look into the school was to help you, as you were left with the whole burden." But, *mea culpa* again; in the rush of the meetings I had omitted to tell her beforehand; now the "pain in her heart" is obstinate.

Is it not strange, though, that the Telugu language has no word for touchiness?

The Mohammedan head mistress turned up. "I cannot

get on with Gnanakshi—she speaks so crossly to the children." I believe it; she has this unfortunate manner with all. And she is the Christian teacher! At that moment Dina herself arrived. She had been away on sick leave. "You are back before your leave is over?" I asked, astonished.

"I cannot stand the ways of my daughter-in-law. I could not remain with my son. But I am too weak to be alone. Will you please make some arrangement for me till I am stronger?" The poor missionary is to work the miracle which a little conciliatoriness would have rendered unnecessary.

"I will send you to our Mission hospital," I said after much thought, "for treatment. But who will take you? Giriamma, you must." Giriamma is her eldest daughter who had brought her mother on this journey.

"My mother-in-law would be vexed if I stayed away longer," began Giriamma. "She is always hard and angry with me. My difficulties are too great to bear; since my husband died very little is earned in our goldsmith business. I have to teach in the school to earn something, then there is the housework when I come back; my son is often ill. If my mother-in-law were kind I could bear all, but now I often think 'if only I were dead.'"

There is real hardship here, poor girl. Her parents-in-law were converts from Hinduism who never really absorbed much Christian teaching. "I will write to your mother-in-law," I said, "and tell her there is no one else to take your mother to hospital; that I urged you to go and she must not blame you when you return."

Remembering Rebekka's complaint, I called Dina back as she was going out. "Do you think Rebekka is rather lonely in Dharmpalli? Her own people are all at Cuddalore. When you get back you might go to see her sometimes and cheer her up a little."

"I will," said Dina, looking a little conscious. She is

really a good and earnest worker, but, like all of us, has her foibles. And to most of us it is easier to be generous than to be just.

I wish they could also be a little generous to me! Salome, another of our Christian women, walked in. I had asked her to come and see me because her eldest daughter Hannah left the Mission school to go to the Government school, where there is no Bible-teaching. "Why have you taken Hannah from the Christian school?"

"Why?" She hesitated, looking this way and that.

"Tell me why," I pressed.

At last it came out. "You took much trouble over Lingamma; you went to their house several times and urged them to let her still come to school and promised to send her for training; you never took any trouble like that over Hannah."

I sat amazed. *Son, thou art always with me.* "Salome, do not our Christian people all know the value of education for their daughters already? You were educated yourself in a Mission school. But Lingamma's people are cowherds, illiterate Hindus; they need teaching, don't they?"

"You visit the Hindus and you do not visit *us*."

I perceive that the reward of entering into other people's lives is to have one's many sins of omission brought home to one. Besides being grateful for this I reflected that if the Christians in St. Paul's time were as easily offended as ours I pitied him in retrospect. Perhaps he did not have so much to do with women, though he had glimpses, no doubt, seeing he besought Euodias and besought Syntyche to be of the same mind. It is a consolation to me that there were ructions among the Christian workers at Philippi—for there certainly are at Andapur!

* * * * *

A more robust trouble has befallen. A special messenger from a distant village came in to say that the teacher there, a lame man, was in fear of assault and robbery. This village is divided into two factions, one composed of the farmers and decent people generally, the other *Boyers*[1] and other lower *Sudras*. These latter are under the thumb of the *Reddi* of Pamurti, who is the terror of that whole countryside, and a scoundrel. Every official knows it; yet he is so cunning that not only can he not be caught himself, but is able to get those who will not bow to his dominion into trouble. Now a murder is said to have taken place in the village. It looks as if the *Reddi* wanted the watchful eyes of the Christian teacher away; for the *Boyers*, doubtless at the *Reddi's* instigation, are advising him to clear out of the village lest his cattle should be injured, his house plundered, and he himself beaten.

* * * * *

Elagunta [the village of the lame teacher]. Here I am at the storm-centre. The scene around is peaceful; the tent is pitched under a tamarind-tree so enormous that it takes the tent as a mushroom would a fly; fields of *ragi* and *gram* surround it; the unoiled wheel of a well rasps the silence somewhat; but solitude is grateful after the distressing scenes this morning.

As far as one can judge by the information from reliable sources, what happened here is, briefly, this. The Pamurti *Reddi* had long borne a grudge against the respectable farmers of Elagunta who would not pay him bribes. In revenge he faked a murder case. A *Yerikela* man under his control was prevailed upon to leave the neighbourhood and disappear. Then, from the corpse of a man dead of fever a hand was cut off and presented as evidence of a crime; the jackals, in this hilly region, being made responsible for the disappearance of the rest.

A charge of murdering the *Yerikela* man who had

[1] Generally field labourers.

disappeared was laid against the farmers. The defence discovered he had once been in jail and sent the hand there to compare thumbmarks. If they were not identical the case would naturally break down. Strange to say, the Pamurti *Reddi* immediately had business in the town of the prison. The jail officials returned the answer: "We have not the thumbmark of this former prisoner and cannot therefore compare it with the hand you sent."

For lack of what would have been decisive evidence for the defence it was not able to hold its own against the many witnesses on the other side, bribed by the *Reddi*. The case went against the farmers and fifteen of them are in jail, a fine coup for the *Reddi*! Two are sentenced for six years, the rest for two, three, and four years.

This morning I was in the homes of these people. In nearly all only women were left; weeping, howling, they stood round me beseeching me to get their men out. They were in dire fear also, for the *Boyers*, emboldened by this tremendous success, are now demanding tribute of everyone in the village. I was told that several merchants had given large amounts of grain sooner than take the risk of being plundered. These poor women have been threatened that their cattle will be stolen, their houses robbed, unless they give more and more bribes. I hope the fact of my visit will help them a little, as the mere rumour of it helped the teacher. For when it leaked out that the teacher had sent a letter enemies guessed it was to the Mission. The *Boyers*, who had been so arrogant before, took fright and asked counsel of their controlling demon, the Pamurti *Reddi*. Immediately the answer was returned that the teacher and his belongings were not to be touched. When further news came that carts were ordered for the missionary cringing *Boyers* bowed before the Christian teacher: "Sir, we hear you want to leave this village? Why should you? No one wishes to harm you; we are all on your side" A curious change of front.

It leads one to guess, however, how differently things might have gone had Christianity and not Hinduism been lord of the whole village instead of only one isolated home.

I tried to put what heart I could into the poor people (all Hindu farmers); they were instructed to take special notice of the names and faces of those blackmailing them; I asked the teacher openly to spread it about in the village that I had inquired who were the people uttering threats. Into whose hands had merchants given grain? The merchants might possibly stand to their witness in court, the women are paralysed by deadly terror. In one house, Asita Reddi's, it was pitiful; there were now only three men-servants with the two little daughters of the house: the eldest of these is about eleven. The mother died two years ago, the father and uncle are in jail. On this child has descended the care of everything; she cooks for all and does the housework. Her little brother of about five goes about nervously sobbing. The weeping and wailing of the grown-ups brought him to that state; the girl of eleven has to mother him as best she can. Up till now there has been a woman servant in the house, but she will not stay. It was her husband who brought the teacher's letter to me. He has not dared to return to the village for fear of ill-treatment; now his wife leaves also. The *dhobies* and the barbers will not work for the relations and servants of the men in jail, afraid of attracting the wrath of the Pamurti *Reddi* and the mishandling of the *Boyers*. The whole thing makes one mad. It is too late to do anything as judgment is already passed; nothing but an appeal to the High Court is left, the cost of which is prohibitive. If the Courts could know the villages themselves, and the oppression exercised by clever scoundrels in powerful positions! I feel sure as regards this case that justice was misinformed, and in consequence miscarried. I am equally convinced that rogues like the Pamurti *Reddi* would never attain to such power among villages where Christianity had taken root. In the first place, Christian teaching effectively works against the fear and weakness which makes such oppression possible; in the second, the Christian teacher is a force with which a hostile village headman learns he has to reckon.

Meanwhile, alone in my tent, more than discouragement assailed. Why were these things allowed to happen?—those lonely children in Asita Reddi's house; the despairing men in jail, knowing their state and their danger; that triumphant blackguard at Pamurti?[1]

In spite of the sunshine, the world around me grew gloomy. Light and assurance failed. Where was God? Old, awful, inward tremors crept up like the waves of a relentless tide. Was He there? Did He care?

Never does the fight for faith cease. And let no one think that missionaries find theirs a less hard one than anyone else does.

But when things were at their darkest, and faith in God and man alike failing, help came. A small thing, but it sufficed. Or was it not small?

> ". . . till that man's heart grows humble and reaches out
> For the last glimmer of the feet of God,
> Grass on the mountain tops. . . ."

It was a little child who led me back that day to where "the least glimmer of the feet of God" shone dimly in the mist.

A small visitor lifted the flap of the tent, the five or six year old daughter in the teacher's home. During the prayer-meeting at their house she had sat and stared unwinking.

1 Some months later he evidently thought it wise to be on the side of the angels, and helped the police to catch a gang of dacoits in the neighbouring hills. For this he was thanked publicly at a meeting in Andapur and presented with a gold-knobbed stick in recognition of his services. The Superintendent of Police said to me on that occasion privately, "Of course we all know he is a scoundrel really. But when he does help us we have to reward him."

Now she stood, tugging at her *dabu*, her little silver belt. Finally she succeeded in unhooking it and presented it to me with a shy smile. Her most precious possession! As it was one of intrinsic value it was impossible, of course, to accept it; but I thanked her and received it temporarily, deeply moved. The impulse of love in a little soul, showing itself in the natural desire to give—human nature was very beautiful after all. And who, but a God of tenderness, could have invented little children?

But to win through life with one's banners of hope and courage flying high to the end is not so simple a matter as I once thought.

> "His soul well knit, and all his battles won,
> Mounts, *and that hardly*, to eternal life."

Matthew Arnold knew what he was talking about.

CHAPTER IX

AMONG THE LOW CASTE

"*Amma, amma! Ho, ammayya!*"

The call, sounded before the dawn, penetrated my slumbers in the upper verandah of my bungalow Sleepily I leaned over the railings. "Who is it?"

"We are *Yerikelas* from Jivapuram."

"What do you want?"

"Grant us a *darshanam*!"

Darshanam means vision, sight—but of whom or what they desired sight remained to be guessed; anyhow it was likely to be a lengthy business. I dressed hurriedly and came down.

They poured forth the old story of injustice and oppression only too frequent in Indian villages.

The *Yerikelas* are a gipsy tribe, of nomad and, one must add, thieving habits. This always renders them liable to special police supervision. Many of them are settling in villages now, acquiring land and trying other means of earning an honest livelihood, such as plaiting mats of split date leaves, weaving blankets of sheep wool, etc. Hinduism counts them almost as low as the outcaste. Between police supervision and caste contempt the path of moral reform is made none too easy for them, resulting in frequent lapses. In our district, as in others, some of them are looking for a friend in the Mission.

This is the story my early callers had to tell.

In their village some waste land adjoined a plot owned by the *Yerikela* headman. It was overrun by prickly-pear. He put in an application for it to the village *Karnam*, the official in charge of land and land records. The *Karnam* assured him it would be granted to him. Thereupon he and others started the immense and tedious labour of clearing the land of the rank growth of this cactus. When it was accomplished he again asked for the assignment. The *Karnam* now declared there had been an oversight, the maps showed that the lands in question adjoined some rich caste man's land on the other side, that he had the first claim on it, and that an application from him had come in also.

The *Yerikela* people were perfectly certain there was no such alignment, and that if the village maps showed it they had been tampered with. But the *Karnam* would not let them see the maps. They therefore desired a sight of the original documents and maps in the Government archives at headquarters. They had come in on the previous day with a man who could read and gone straight to the Government office with their request. But being considered low caste they had not ventured to go in. They waited outside the gate, calling to all who passed in, "Grant us a *darshanam*!"

But no one troubled to inquire their business; perhaps one could hardly expect it of busy officials going to their routine work. The simple villagers did not know whom to ask, the afternoon passed into evening, the gates of the Government office were closed without their being any nearer to the desired *darshanam*.

That was the reason they had come before it was light, to make sure of catching me at home.

I cycled round to the house of the Public Prosecutor—luckily a friend—to inquire the rights of the matter.

"Everybody has the right to see the maps of his town or village," the official explained. "It is shocking the way these poor people are put upon. I am glad you came; if you will send them on to me I will see them through."

So they got their *darshanam*, also the proof of the *Karnam's* deceit, and went back, heartened for further fight.

But it is a long fight. Fears and inherited bad tendencies within (such as love of adventure and night-raids on cattle and sheep and fowls), foes without, in the shape of police and of caste people. It is hard to see how without a strong motive force as well as a strong friend—both of which may be found in Christianity—they will ever be integrated into the general community as useful citizens.

And harder still is it for those yet a grade below them, the regular outcastes, in reality the original inhabitants and owners of the land of which Aryan invasion deprived them, forcing them into serfdom.

Much has been written about their pitiable state, and yet few who have not been to India (and by no means all who have) realize the difficulties of their lives. I can only throw a few sidelights here, by narrating some personal experiences of my own and of neighbouring missionaries.

In Konneru a *Mala*[1] family in dire poverty had borrowed a small sum from a Mohammedan moneylender, promising their son as security; an ordinary custom. Of course they could never repay; moneylenders cunningly refuse instalments, demanding the lump sum, together with the interest which has accumulated at an exorbitant rate. (An anna in the rupee per month, which works out at 75 per cent. per annum, is considered moderate.) When the boy was old enough to be useful he was taken by the Mohammedan into his household, practically as a slave. He worked for this master for years, while the poor parents would have been thankful for his labour and support. Then our Bible-woman, Bhagyamma, settled in the neighbourhood. On her visit to this village she found out the state of affairs. The brave old woman straightway went to the moneylender and boldly demanded the release of the youth, telling the man what he knew to be the truth, that he had no legal right to keep the lad. She actually cowed him into giving the youth his liberty. Ultimately the family became Christians. When the Mohammedan wanted work done in his fields he called the lad, now named Samuel, whom he had found to be a good worker, to do it, paying him regular wages.

[1] A section of Telugu outcastes.

"It is the same kind of miracle as God worked with Elijah," said the grateful parents when I came to the village.

"Whatever do you mean?" I asked.

"Well, was he not fed by crows? Is not a crow a thief-bird, stealing and grabbing from everybody? Just like a moneylender. But now God makes the selfish moneylender feed us by paying our son wages."

Here was a strange modern raven and a new version of the miracle.

But would it have happened apart from Christianity?

In a neighbouring district where the Mission is carrying on a large work among the outcastes some Pariah [1] families who had become Christians owned some land near their village. The caste people, bitterly opposed to their conversion and showing their enmity by every possible means, deliberately drove their cattle into the growing crops of the outcastes. The only remedy anyone has against stray cattle doing damage of this kind is to catch the offending animals and take them to the Pound, where the owner has to redeem them on payment of a fine. It is a troublesome business at the best, but in this case it was quite hopeless as the manager of the Pound was himself the owner of the cattle devastating the outcastes' corn. One of the Christians took heart of grace to withstand the outrage; he drove off the cattle from his fields and prepared to keep guard against further invasion.

This enraged the caste people. A Pariah standing up to them? He must be taught a lesson. They formed a party and, armed with sticks and clubs, set upon him together, bore him down and beat him mercilessly.

The Christians dispatched a hasty messenger to the missionary, begging him to come. He was found returning from a morning's tour among other villages, but when he heard of that morning's doings he turned his car straight round and drove off to the scene (not so simple a matter as

[1] A section of Tamil outcastes.

it sounds, as a good deal of the way lay over a track no motor had ever been over and never intended for one). Medical advice and evidence were obtained for the sufferer, who was found prostrate and covered with weals and bruises. Evidence of the assault was taken from eye-witnesses.

"Will you stand to this in court?" they were asked.

"Sir, how can we? The chief caste man is so powerful he can get any number of witnesses on his side. Our lives would not be safe if we went against him. He has been known to get people murdered who stood in his way. Of course, in such a way that it could not be proved."

The beaten man himself, however, showed remarkable courage. "I will take a court case against them," he resolved firmly.

However averse to the principle of Christians going to law for settlement of quarrels, the missionary felt that under such conditions of intimidation and oppression the only way was to nurse this spark of manhood. A whole community was being terrorized and robbed; the people had no redress; slavery had invaded their very souls. But now, on that inner battle-ground, the new spirit which had come with the advent of Jesus Christ among them, withstood the age-long habit of abject submissiveness; in saying he would fight, this Pariah was surely climbing the first rung of that ladder of the ascent of man, which is to bring all mankind to their ultimate heritage of ruling the earth by laws and powers of the spirit—a heritage few have even envisaged yet.

These poor people's first and desperate need was freedom, a sense of inner freedom, of not being slaves, compelled to endure any injustice and condemned to hopelessness.

Difficult days followed. The new course of resistance was fraught with peril, and well the outcastes knew it. But the complaint was bravely made, the case lodged. The mere fact of Pariahs taking out a case against them was in itself an affront disgracing the caste men concerned in the eyes of others. Naturally, plans of revenge were brewing. The Pariahs heard it and trembled. Not one of them dared to go along the public road. Even the Christian teacher, though a strong and independent man, only ventured to go to and from the village by a circuitous route. To this day he dare not wear a coat in the presence of caste people of this village. He knows what might follow. Intimidations and threats went on freely. Money is a powerful factor, and to poverty-stricken Pariahs the offer of large sums to induce them to withhold or alter evidence in court must have been no small temptation. Refusals were met by dire threats. A man fled in terror to the missionary saying his life was no longer safe; the chief caste man had threatened to kill him if he gave evidence—what was he to do?

The case was fixed for a certain date. The plaintiff and his witnesses walked the twenty-odd miles to the court; for all of them the excursion meant the loss of the day's, and probably the next day's, labour. On arrival at the court they were informed that the case had been postponed ten days. They had to return to their village and come again on the newly-fixed date. Then the same thing happened. No less than six times did they take that journey in vain; no compensation of any kind was given for their loss of time and wages and labour, let alone the mental effect of becoming dispirited. Whether this was a move inspired by the defendants, or—as is often the case—the careless ways of Indian officials, I do not know.

At last, however, the case had to be heard, and the result spelt a triumph for the outcastes. The assaulters were fined 150 rupees or two months' jail. The Indian magistrate, knowing his country, said afterwards, "The end of this case is not yet." He knew with what extraordinary tenacity grudges are stored and a return blow given, maybe, years after.

At the time of writing—for this case is quite recent—the caste people of the village in question are still biding their time. But meanwhile a new thing is being talked of with amazement in the villages of those parts: a Pariah has rights!

Not always have unjustly-treated Pariahs been successful in their appeal to law. In the army no distinction is allowed. A number of Pariahs have become sepoys. A Christian sepoy of Pariah origin went on leave to his village during an outbreak of plague. Before travelling back he had to get his plague passport signed by the village headman. He went on this errand dressed in full uniform, with boots, putties, coat, and turban. The headman, seeing the Pariah thus arrayed, was enraged and went to beat him. The sepoy fled to his house and locked himself in. The headman's party came down and tried to force their way into the house. The sepoy's wife went out to them and pleaded for her husband. They seized her and flogged her, cutting her breasts open with the cane they used. The missionary who told me these facts saw the woman and her wounds himself. The husband was also seized and beaten—for the offence of appearing before caste people in a coat. The case was taken to court. It was postponed more than a dozen times, causing the plaintiff and witnesses enormous inconvenience. In the end the case was practically dismissed.

A Christian Pariah boy, brought up and educated in a missionary boarding-home, was home for his holidays. He, too, had to get his plague passport signed by the headman. Taught self-respect in the Mission and the way to appear before elders and superiors, he went to the headman nicely dressed and wearing a coat. This headman also was furious at the sight, had him seized and cruelly flogged; his coat was torn off and ripped to pieces.

That boy got back his own in a different way. When his education was finished he emigrated to the Straits Settlements, where he ultimately obtained a very good position and was generally esteemed. When he last visited India and went to his own village even the headman treated him with respect. In the Pariah quarters of that village the Mission has now a very good school to which caste boys also come, amongst them a son of that headman himself!

In another village where the Pariahs came under the influence of Christianity and where many of them became baptized the headman and others persecuted them in every possible way. Their livelihood, i.e. field labour for the caste people, was taken away; they were not even allowed firewood. When this did not avail to make them revert to Hinduism the headman had their houses set on fire and burnt. This, however, was proved against him and he went to prison for six months. When he came out he pursued his old tactics, caused the Pariahs to be robbed of their goats and injured in all possible ways, but managed to avoid legal detection. Some of the Pariahs, almost starving, recanted. Finally, however, they all returned to Christianity; their teacher worked on faithfully and courageously, and to-day the Pariah school is largely attended by caste boys. The Pariahs, as Christians, have continued to gain general respect.

It is difficult within a limited compass to give a true picture. The instances quoted, though they could be multiplied, must not lead anyone to think the problem is solved. Even Gandhi, admitting them to his own Ashram in these days, has not solved it.

There are over sixty millions of outcastes in India. Christian Missions have barely touched the fringe of them. Reformers are agitating; Government is investigating and willing to help by grants of land, etc., yet for the bulk of the outcaste population the old conditions of oppression and injustice remain.

Wanted: neighbours.

Here and there they may be found. Lachmi Nursappa,

the Brahmin priest of Patacheruvu, who championed the cause of the outcastes in his town, has been mentioned elsewhere.[1] He has passed to his reward, but another heroic figure in this district is still with us, Bhumanand Reddi of Vajrapad. He came under the influence of a Lingait priest who was baptized as a Christian. Nanjandappa,[2] a lover of his kind and of all who are oppressed, infected his friend with his own enthusiasm; Bhumanand Reddi became an out and out social reformer. A great outcry was made, also attempts to ruin him in various ways, but Bhumanand is wealthy and can afford to disregard opposition and contempt. Outcastes are received at the house of this dignified old man, of fine and wise countenance; if marriages can be arranged for young widows on Brahmo Samaj lines he lends his house for the ceremony and pays expenses; he helps to educate backward and low-caste boys. His own daughter, a child widow, he encouraged to re-marry, but she preferred to remain with her father and help in his work. Much loneliness must of necessity be the portion of the inmates of such a home, still within the pale of Hinduism, yet surely treading in the footsteps of the greatest Lover of men ever known in human history.

But though there are these amazing and honoured exceptions, in the main it still remains true to say that among the general population lack of neighbourliness for the outcaste troubles no one. They may be denied justice, deprived of land and of water, of the right to dress as others dress, of the use of roads—who cares? They are outside the pale of respectable society.

And if recently Hinduism has woken up to the fact that this lowest stratum of Indian society shows signs of insubordination, of going over to other religions where they shall count as brothers and human beings, and has now decreed that outcastes are part of the Hindu community,

[1] *An Uphill Road in India.*
[2] See Chap. xvii. A Solitary.

what has actuated that act of belated and still very scanty justice?

Though it is never very safe to judge other people's motives one cannot but think that what moved them was not love, but fear. Not care for the oppressed (although, again, there is no knowing how far they have unconsciously been influenced by example of Jesus Christ), but alarm lest the secession of outcastes in still greater numbers should shake the whole body of Hinduism to its foundations.

But the day when it will be so shaken is on its way all the same. Tunnels are being dug in that great mountain in unexpected places. Take the story of Nillur.

The village of Nillur had been one of our failures. (The story is described elsewhere in detail.[1]) It was one of the first in our district where outcastes became interested in Christianity, and the very first whence two Mala girls went for further education to a boarding-home. Alas, when cholera broke out one of these two fell a victim. The people were terrified and took it as a punishment of the gods for forsaking the old ways. An elder whose wise words had always influenced the people for good and who might have soothed away their fears had passed away shortly before. The scare caused by the girl's death and the absence of the old headman's good counsel caused the people to revert to their old worship; the school was empty, no one came to prayers any more, the teacher had to leave and the ancient idols were set up again in their shrine.

But one person remained steadfast, the widowed mother of the other girl. Till then I had never thought much of Martha, a woman with a tongue! Conversation with her was a thing to be avoided, I had learned by bitter experience. But now it turned out that grumbles and complaints and fits of temper had hidden a rather fine independence of spirit.

"Yes, they are all going back," she announced, "but I am

[1] *A Struggle for a Soul*, Chap. Shadow.

not. They are all telling me not to send Krupi back to school, 'the Mother' will kill her too, they say—but I shall send her back. We shall go on praying to *Yesu Swami*."

She kept to her resolve—a heroic one under those circumstances—Krupi's education went on, and no vengeance of the cholera goddess overtook the village for this defiance. In fact, for several years the place remained singularly free from this scourge.

"See how wise we were to return to the old ways," said the Malas of Nillur. "*Her* wrath is appeased. It is not safe for us to worship the white people's gods."

Krupi came home during holidays and tried in vain to make a more friendly atmosphere. Now and then she went on visits to relations in a village called Cherlopalli, and there her stories of what she had learned at school were more willingly received. Particularly the many lyrics she had learned to sing, made a great impression. When she had little groups of listeners round her at sunset, singing to them these Indian melodies and explaining the words, caste people passing near the low-caste quarters stood still to listen. They even took to coming over on purpose.

"Where does that girl come from?" they asked.

"Nillur," was the answer.

"But a Mala girl? Look at her sense! Behold her nice manners, and the wisdom she has learned! How did she learn it?"

"The Mission people had a school at her village," someone said.

The caste people shook their heads. They knew little or nothing of the Mission. But this girl! "She knows more than *our* girls," said the villagers; "she has more sense, her ways are better ways. What school was that at Nillur?"

And then, one morning, knowing nothing of all this, or that the Nillur Malas had relations in Cherlopalli, or that Krupi had visited there, simply because I happened to be in camp in the neighbourhood, I went to Cherlopalli. A farmer on his way to work accosted me and asked the usual friendly question of the Indian road: "Where do you come from?"

"Andapur."

"What is your work?"

"I belong to the Mission."

He turned round and walked back with me. "You belong to the Mission? Will you put a school in our village?"

"But there is a school in the village just over the river. It is not far. Can your children not go there?"

"But that is a Hindu school. I mean *your* school. You know the teaching you taught in Nillur? I want that teaching. If you will only put a school here and teach like the Mission school in Nillur I will send my three sons."

The Mission school in Nillur! The words recalled a heartbreak. The building was falling to pieces; no teacher there, nor scholars; the people gone back to crudest idol worship. Moreover, in its best days it had been a school for outcastes, and this man was a caste man. I was frankly puzzled.

"What do they call you?" I asked my companion.

"Chinappa Naidu. Many of us would like a school where our children can be taught like they taught Krupi in Nillur."

"What Krupi?"

"Nillur Krupi." Then the connection dawned upon me. My companion rambled on. "You would not think she was a Mala girl. Much wisdom had they taught her in the Mission school. She was clean and wore tidy clothes, she said words of wisdom every evening. Many of us caste people came to listen. Yes, a Brahmin widow also. She sang many lyrics; we all liked them; we should like our children to learn them, and all those good ways that Mala girl had learned. Therefore give us a school like the Mala school in Nillur."

It was really the boarding-school which had taught Krupi

what so impressed the caste people of Cherlopalli—but the point is that they *were* impressed. That which could raise an ignorant and despised outcaste child to a state of dignity and influence where others listened to her with respect—"that teaching," whatever it was, "we want that for our children."

Chinappa Naidu was asking more than he knew.

But will not all India be asking it in the future?

CHAPTER X

VISITORS

A Governor's visit is upon us. Andapur is convulsing itself in preparations. Roads are being mended (for which reason the bicycle and I could wish His Excellency to favour us every year); bamboo poles—on which will presently blossom papered archways with welcoming inscriptions—stick up untidily along roadsides, public buildings are being whitewashed, the places for foundation-stones are being levelled. Functions are being planned, though many arrangements seem to be left to the inspiration of the moment—an unreliable factor to my Western mind. An official came round and mentioned to me conversationally, "Your girls are to do a *Kolatum*[1] at the Public Welcome." Now schools have been closed on account of an outbreak of cholera and are scarcely in order again yet; a little previous practice seems advisable, but no written communication followed the verbal message. Not sharing India's faith in the efficacy of requests sent at the last minute I wrote to the Deputy Collector to inquire what was wanted. From the condescending tone of the reply it was evident he thought I was anxious for the Mission schools to be in evidence: "I will arrange it if you wish." To my hasty note that I should be only too thankful to be saved the trouble the peremptory answer came that it was all fixed.

A *peon* appeared with the formal note of invitation to the official dinner, "to meet Their Excellencies," to which the usual formula of accepting with much pleasure was returned; later on in private conversation an inquiry was made whether this was obligatory for one who was not a lover of functions. My hostess kindly assured me that I was dispensable, but when further discussion revealed the fact that there would

[1] A kind of folk-dance.

be thirteen at table the whole of Andapur high society decreed there must be a fourteenth. Yet a few minutes later we were all smiling at the story of a subordinate in someone's office who had given as his excuse for joining duty a day late the fact that on starting for Andapur he had met a widow carrying glowing charcoal in a pan. A widow was bad enough, but one carrying fire! The start could not be risked on such an unlucky day.

The hot weather has given way to monsoon clouds and greyness. Whenever I get the chance I garden strenuously. Zinnias are in bloom, cosmos and convolvuli are coming up. I am now aspiring to grass, real grass; not the common stuff with vicious spears of which the compound is full. Sods of turf are being dug from a stream-bed a mile away and carted here; the lawn that is being created with these is at present a mountainous region of great crevasses, owing to the uneven thickness of the sods, as well as the infinite variety of their shapes; you could not have tea there if you valued your ankles or your china, but it looks gratefully green to the eye in our still parched and yellow plains.

Unfortunately not only to my eye. The recently acquired cow is a standing menace to the garden; the creature is of a greediness beyond belief. Kitchen towels hung out to dry are not safe from her—I could bear that—but directly she arrived she ate down my cherished cork-trees. Then they were enclosed with thorns, recovered and sprouted again. The thorn-hedge had spikes an inch and a half long and was staked so close together that a crocodile would have shrunk from forcing a passage, but this degenerate cow got through and ate the trees again.

"You must choose," said the collector's wife, catching me in the act of shrieking with rage at the vandalism, "between that cow and the cork-trees."

But like Jane of old I hanker after both. Wire-netting is on the way, also the miscreant cow's head will now be tethered to its leg, an Indian fashion which points out the way of bovine righteousness clearly: grass, not trees.

I used to think it a rather cruel mode of education, but evidently India knows her cows. Humbly I learn from her. But now the creature has become filled with yearnings for space! The twenty-seven acres of this compound do not suffice her; she roams the wide South Indian plain, thereby causing much diversion in the domestic establishment, whose joy it is to disperse in all directions: "The cow has gone!" One would think that maternal feelings would restrain such excursiveness; her calf bellows and bellows, but nothing cares this mammal, off she marches to satisfy her voracity. Between greed, thick-skinnedness, and heartlessness, I do not like that cow.

Perhaps she sensed unfriendliness and desired to do me a tort in turn. Into a midday rest broke the sound of munching from the garden. The unspeakable animal had broken its rope and leaped the barrier. India has touching confidence in ropes, and ties up almost anything with them, shafts, wheels, doors, motor-cars, animals, etc., but my trust in ropes has been destroyed for ever by this quadruped. Two beds of cosmos about to flower have gone, all the zinnias, and a whole hibiscus-bush! No thought of the West learning patience from the East restrained me, British intolerance oozed from every pore as I pelted her with stones out of the garden. Valiant galloping saved her from hearing further expressions of what I thought of her; Venkappa, the cowman, peacefully slumbering in the verandah, was less lucky.

To appease me he is now seeking strenuously to fulfil such orders as he can comply with with less fatigue—"Show me the milk," is a standing one. To my own undoing! For people come to see me from the earliest beginnings of the day; in the middle of an interview Venkappa appears, stretching forth a foaming tin; I wave him away, he waits faithfully round the corner. Released from my visitor, I rush off to the next job—after me he stalks with the milk, till I become like Coleridge's nervous individual in the country lane who

> "Turns no more his head,
> Because he knows a frightful fiend
> Doth close behind him tread."

He suggested now a coolie watching the cow—"while I eat my rice," he insinuated; and added resourcefully, "I have brought a female."

"Who is she?" I asked. "Young or old?"

"Young."

"Is she a married woman?"

"Married."

"To whom? Is it a respectable family?"

He hummed and hawed. "She is a female," he insisted, and seemed quite certain about that, anyhow. In the end it dawned on my obtuseness that it was his wife!

Returning from *Kolatum* practice with excited schoolgirls, I was met at the bungalow by sounds of awful shrieks and a hasty rushing of all available clans from neighbouring compounds towards the well in mine. Dorcas detached herself from the wailing multitude and tore towards me, "Please come! Nursana has fallen into the well and is 'all sorts.' " (The vernacular idiom meaning "very bad.") At the same moment I espied two Indian gentlemen approaching from the gate. It was the very day before the Governor was to arrive and visitors were only too likely.

"Will you please excuse me for a few minutes?" I called out to them. " A man has fallen into the well."

They hastened near. It was my friend Mr. Rangavachari, the lawyer, and a stranger. Mr. Rangavachari, whom no occasion finds anything but a gentleman, said instantly, "May we come too? Perhaps we can help."

We found a gory spectacle; evidently Nursana's turban

had fallen into the well (for something is still floating down there—oh, my drinking water!) and he had climbed down after it; the rope he held on to broke (what did I say?); on the rocks below he knocked various holes into himself and looked affrighting. Eventually, washed and bandaged, he was sent off to hospital, Venkappa driving the cart, the house-servant supporting the patient, who felt faint; as the cook was already away, indulging in gossip in the bazar, the whole staff was now gone and showed no sign of returning. The cow was left to follow the dictates of that pilgrim soul of hers, while my Indian visitors and I talked in the verandah on the problems of the universe.

The other man was Mr. Nilkanta Rao, the detective in His Excellency's suite. The talk turned, as so often in India, on matters philosophical and religious. Mr. Nilkanta Rao had been educated in a Mission college, and expressed the view that Hinduism will learn all it can from Christianity and after casting off its ancient encrustations will become, with the Christian addition, the perfect religion. This was very interesting and occupied us for two hours, when the servants returned with the news that Nursana had lost two teeth, but otherwise would be all right presently. "It's an ill wind," etc. The Andapur doctor had been yearning for a patient to fill the last vacant bed in our hospital before Their Excellencies inspect it to-morrow; the servants could not say enough about the enthusiasm with which Nursana had been welcomed, and the kindness with which his unwillingness to stay had been overcome.

* * * * *

We are through with our day of functions; two foundation-stones were well and truly laid, the schoolgirls made a creditable show at the appointed moment, and Their Excellencies said kind words to a relieved manager. A "surprise visit" was paid to a village, but it was not the villagers who got the surprise. I did not (oh my ill-luck!) see it myself, but was told of two Welcome arches along the road; one bearing the entirely correct expression of loyal and pious sentiment, "God bless His Excellency," the second holding sentiment as loyal and pious, though startling to English ears, "God help Her Excellency"!

In the late afternoon, when visitors and townspeople alike were straggling across the market-place from one function in the Town Hall to another in the hospital, the Indian Head mistress of a girls' school pulled my sleeve, "Ask Her Excellency to come to our school to-morrow."

"Certainly," our visitor kindly acceded; "and to yours too."

Help! In honour of the occasion a holiday had been arranged for the next day; with a sinking heart I thought of the general untidiness. How to prepare now? Casting round appealing eyes a schoolgirl was spied in the crowd.

"Run, *run*! Tell our head mistress, tell the conductress, Her Excellency is coming to our school in the morning! All girls to be present. Run!"

For none of the usual festive preparations was there time; it was a school in very workaday garb that met the guest of honour; no flags and but few garlands. But the street outside made up in interest! It was bursting with excitement. Spectators poured into the school after us; the police would have stopped them, but "Let them come; let, anyhow, all women come," ordered the friendly visitor. So in they came, friends and neighbours, among them Brahmin widows in their red *saris*, Sudras also, till there was not room for any more.

"How many of you can read?" asked Her Excellency.

Among that crowd of perhaps forty women only two could, so she spoke to them a little on education for girls, in English of course, which was presently translated. But words went for little that morning, the women were all taken up with gazing.

"That she came so near! That we could see her quite close and unhurried!" were their comments afterwards. Specially touching were the whispers of some widows: "Thank you, thank you for bringing her, and for letting *us* come!" For a tendency to exclude widows, whom India shuts out from every auspicious or festive occasion, had been noted and quelled.

"I have enjoyed this more than many a ceremonial visit to other schools," was the gracious comment of Her Excellency in private later on. There spoke, one felt, the heart of a fine and motherly Englishwoman, glad of contact with the people. Perhaps East and West are not so very far apart after all—in the hearts of women, anyhow, meeting does not seem impossible. The trouble is officialdom, accentuated by barriers of language. It is difficult to know how to overcome it; stateliness and ceremonial have their place; the awe and reverence they help to engender are great qualities—woe to the community or nation whence they have fled!

Some of these thoughts were in the background of my mind during the official dinner-party. That the refreshing youth on one side of me had only just come to India was proved by his inquiry, "What are *cheetahs*?" Further, he wanted to know the difference between leopards and panthers, flooring me immediately. I knew that leopards had spots, but my authority said nothing about panthers. Others came to the rescue with the information that it was chiefly a matter of difference in size. None of us were uncomfortably learned; when talk drifted on to Hyder Ali and the Battle of Plassy none of us could remember the date.

A curious sense came over me in the company of these white men and women, rulers of India—of their atmosphere; so British, so kind, so tolerant, so just, so full of that hidden force of character which makes them the fine rulers that they are. But it also contained an element of aloofness.

"What do the Indians read?" the Governor asked me in the little interview accorded to each guest after dinner. The vagueness and vastness of the question staggered me. A saving memory of a recent visitor flashed across me.

"A man in Your Excellency's suite is a careful student of the works of Sir Oliver Lodge," I replied.

"Really? Who is that?"

"Nilkanta Rao."

"Who is he?"

"The detective."

By that time carriages were ready to take us to the Town Hall, where conjuring tricks and fireworks were further to entertain our guests. One of the magician's items was to ask the Governor to write down a word. He then looked round and happening to catch my eye proffered a similar request. His Excellency looked laughingly across and said, "I cannot think of any words." I was in like predicament. Finally, however, he did write one. Then a word flashed to me with such certainty that it seemed the only word in the universe. I wrote it. The writers then folded their papers and held them in their closed palms; the magician touched their wrists and one by one stated the letters of the written words till he had them complete. Thought transference? Why not? Was not the same mysterious process responsible for the Governor's word being *sword*, and mine *victory*? And was it not thought transference to a more mediate degree, i.e. the subtle British atmosphere in our minds, that these words were chosen? Two Indians would hardly have written them.

It is not easy for East and West to meet. Her Excellency had confessed to a great desire to get quietly into the villages and see people as they ordinarily live. But officialdom comes in, preparations have to be made, roads lined with police, etc.; by the time she arrives all wear metaphorical and uninteresting Sunday clothes.

"Would Your Excellency care to visit an Indian home to-morrow, after the schools?" I offered. "Quite near by, where no extra road police would be needed?"

"Yes, very much."

A hasty message was dispatched to the house of some Indian friends. Would it be convenient for the Governor's wife to come into their house for a few minutes? Quite informally, just to see an Indian home.

Alack and alas! the reply came, "Greatly regret, it is not convenient."

India, sensitive and suspicious, could not think what this extraordinary approach meant. Just a little ordinary friendliness was hard to believe in. For the Great Ones suitable preparations must be made, the place swept and garnished, garlands in readiness. "But Her Excellency did not want any of that," I explained afterwards; "she wished to see you as you always are and your house as it always is."

Great were the regrets when they at length understood this, and—as regrets for lost opportunities always are—wholly vain; the visitors had gone by then.

CHAPTER XI

AT FESTIVAL TIME

It is *Dassera* time, the festival of Kali; "ten nights" its name denotes. Andapur town looks gay; women go about in their brightest and best *saris*; the streets are thronged with festive people on their way to temples or to visit friends and inspect their *Dassera* tables. For in every house a table or little platform is set up, with receding shelves like stairs, covered with white cloth; on these are displayed models of whatever happens to be the family occupation; of household vessels; of farming, weaving, spinning, etc., implements; school books and toys of the children; account books of the merchant, and so on; the idea being to obtain for these their works the divine blessing for the coming year. It is a very beautiful idea, this recognition that the blessing of God is needed for common daily and earthly tasks—may it be remembered by many hearts in the town! But beautiful ideas underlying religious rites are apt to be forgotten, in India as well as in the West, and in practice, nowadays, the *Dassera* table causes great rivalry and open ambition to have the best one. All sorts of costly and pretty things, having nothing to do with the family calling, are placed on the shelves and pointed out with satisfaction to chagrined sightseers, who have not anything so valuable to show when the return visit is made. Their dear human nature! I should, I am certain, feel exactly like that myself if we missionaries took to having, say, Christmas tables and had to place on them models of the works and operations in our respective stations. Awful thought!

I was reminded of the spirit of rivalry recently when I walked through the bazar; a woman plucked at my sleeve and, evidently in anticipation of *Dassera*, whispered urgently, "Can you, will you, give me an eye-shutting doll? I will pay for it. Please give." An English doll performing that entrancing trick would, of course, be *facile princeps* among common and local exhibitions. Yet the white visitor is fascinated by these same common and local models—thus do we all desire the magic of the New and Strange and the Far Away.

This afternoon I walked through the gay and festive bazar street and smiled with the people at the passing shows; one was a little cart, drawn by a goat, its horns wreathed with flowers; a tiny boy and girl sat in the cart, dressed like Solomon in all his glory and hung all over with jewels and flowers; they sat proud and immovable like little idols, rather a darling little show, though the boy leading the goat pestered for *pice*. The people laughed and gave to him and waved to the children; everyone looked smiling and happy; the dazzling sunlight flooded the street and would have made the dullest colours radiant, and already there was far other than dullness. The East knows how to take its holidays! Leisure and charming gaiety come to it more gracefully than to the frantically busy West. As I walked through the sunny street I could not help sympathizing with the sense of merry-making and festivity which pervaded it, but in reality my thoughts were far from joy, for it was sorrow that had brought me. "Come and see our table!" called an acquaintance from her door.

I shook my head. "Afterwards, afterwards," I promised. "Someone is in trouble. I must go there first."

When I arrived at my destination the door of the house was shut. No women in gorgeous robes lounged on the *pial*. No children played near; no flowers were visible. The fourth and only remaining son of the house had died the evening before. Silently and vainly the sunshine rested on the mud wall. I knocked.

"Who is there?" I could hear someone ask from inside.

"May I come in?" I asked hesitatingly. "It is I, Missiamma. May I enter?"

"Come," said a tired voice.

I pushed the door open. After the glare in the streets I could at first distinguish nothing in the windowless and dark interior; but presently perceived a curtain drawn right across the room. From behind it came the sound of weeping. I stole round.

The poor bereaved mother sat on the floor, her *sari* drawn over her face, evidently so worn out with grief that there was no strength left for the usual noisy demonstrations of sorrow which Hindu etiquette demands. She spoke no word of greeting. Two other women, relations, sat by her. All three were weeping quietly, hopelessly.

I sat down by them on the floor, my own heart over-full, yet conscious of utter helplessness. In the face of such sorrow, confronted by the awful mystery of Death—how bring consolation? The finality, the terrible finality of death, as it must appear to this poor Hindu mother—as indeed, it must appear to us all—overpowered me. Words would not come. I could force no phrases over my lips. In silence I sat with them, inwardly groping and praying for help. For if Christ's coming means anything at all it surely means that God does not mean any of His children to be plunged in hopeless despair when death closes the door on the sight and touch of a loved one. Ah, if Christ would only come Himself and say something comforting to these poor people! I sighed. "*Lord, if Thou hadst been here . . .!*"

The old cry. My heart re-echoed it in that sorrow-laden silence. Perhaps now, as then, human grief would have moved Him to tears.

"God cares!" burst from me. "Amma, God cares for you!"

Slowly the *sari* was withdrawn from the mother's ravaged face and she spoke.

"How can God care for me? He has taken my son."

"Wait," I besought, "wait and find out."

For suddenly that wonderful sonnet of Blanco White's had flashed into my mind and words came.

"Rutnamma, round you it is now night. Black, hopeless night. The dark is always full of terrors. Suppose a child had never seen the night, never been outside after dark. And suppose it happened that the child was left alone outside one day and saw the sun set and the light fade. What fear and terror would fill the little mind. As far as it knew it had never been dark before, like this. But after a while, something new appeared. In the blackness overhead a star shone out. A light, in the fearful darkness a light! And presently, more and more lights, countless lights, the whole sky full of them. Would not the little child forget its terror? Might it not say, 'Why did I never see them before?' If we went outside now, Rutnamma, should we see them in this midday? Not a single one. The sun hides them. But will you stand outside to-night? And as you see the stars come out will you remember that the dark has its own lights which we never could find out in the day? Daylight deceives. Night holds new truth. So does the night of sorrow round you now. Amma, God has stars for the dark! God has a secret which He cannot whisper to your heart except in grief. He knows this way you have to take. Wait and feel Him beside you."

"We never heard such high words," broke out one of the relations. "Do you think we think such high thoughts? All we do is to weep and tear our hair and say, 'Gone, gone.' When we think of our gods is it any comfort? We are angry with them. We say, 'we have brought you flowers, we have worshipped you, we have broken you coconuts and strewn camphor and done all those meritorious things, and you do thus to us!' And we curse them. How can we think high things like you are saying? They are too high for us."

"All of us can only learn them slowly; but believe me, amma, God has stars for the dark," I repeated.

The mother gave me a look of utter hopelessness. "Think of God, you say," she murmured drearily. "If only I had *not* thought of Him! I wish I had not prayed to Him so often."

"What do you mean?" I asked, astonished. "Surely it is always well for us to think of God."

Sorrowfully she shook her head. "No, it is not well. For when you think of God it makes Him think of you. Then He remembers your sins. And takes away your son. Oh, I have thought of him!" she cried. "I wanted to preserve my last son. I prayed, every time I woke in the night I prayed. I knew I must get some merit, so I fasted often. Once for a whole month I went without salt in my food. I thought it might count. But because I remembered God He remembered me. He counts our sins when He thinks of us. If only I had not thought of Him! He might have forgotten me. He might have overlooked me, and my son might be alive."

"You mistake, you grievously mistake, amma!" I cried. "*Not weighing our merits, but pardoning our offences.* That is His thought towards us."

Could the distortion of the divine Image, could human despair go further? Religion, the very thing that Hindu mother turned to for consolation, becoming a two-edged sword as she clung to it!

"*Hallowed be Thy Name.* Recognized, understood, and beloved be Thy Name and Nature!" my heart cried, as I searched for words to bring a truer conception of God to this despairing heart.

They sat very still, listening. "The time of grief is the time of His visitation," I concluded. "He will speak to you if you will listen. Do not miss His voice!"

They sat rather awestruck and seemed to think they would hear a voice that very moment.

"In your hearts," I repeated. "To every waiting heart He comes. *A broken and a contrite heart He will not despise.*"

And then I passed out into the glare and gaiety of the street again, into the noise and laughter and the talk of good food, and had to admire the *Dassera* tables of several Hindu friends. But my thoughts remained in the shadow behind the curtain, with those hearts in bitter sorrow, waiting for the coming of His Feet.

The sun was setting in splendour over the rice-fields as I walked home at last. The first star appeared. When I reached the bungalow night had fallen. I glanced up and saw the whole sky aglow, alive with those stars which God has for the dark.

CHAPTER XII

IN VILLAGES AND TOWNS

AT the little country station I walked into the one and only office to book my camp luggage. The Assistant Station Master, in charge during the day, sat there holding his head with both hands and seemed unable to take in what I said.

"Are you ill?" I asked.

"Oh, Madam, if I could cut my throat it would be better! The pain, the pain!" He produced the ticket.

"Can you not take sick leave?"

"If you asked for a year they would not give it." I supposed that requests take time to go through. Or was this hard-heartedness the result of sick leave being asked too often in out of the way places?

The demand for a bicycle ticket seemed to drive him frantic.

"*Ayyo, ayyo!*"[1] he wailed, searching for the book. When he had found it his voice grew more hollow and sepulchral.

"Oh, Madam, I have not even washed my face. . . . Name, please? . . . No, I have not washed. I hoped that would keep the pain away. . . . To Makaji? . . . When I have the pain I am not a man—*ayyo—ayyo!*" I felt he was coming to pieces before my eyes.

"Have you been to the dispensary?"

"Yes, he painted something on, but that is only good for people who eat tamarinds, not for me. I ought to sleep till sunrise, *ayyo!* but the mail comes past at five. The water in this place does not suit me; I have no friends here or any relations to look after me. I had to send my wife to her home for her confinement, my difficulties are too great."

The crowd at the window was growing clamorous. "Ticket, Sarr, ticket!"

[1] Alas! or oh dear!

Distractedly he punched some. "Give me the right money," he moaned.

"We did! It is only four and a half annas to Dodduru."

He banged it down in despair and grasped his head. "Not right, not right," he groaned. A whistle sounded in the distance. The porter rushed in. "Bell, Sir?"

"Tell someone to take the bicycle." He turned pleadingly to me.

"I will see to it myself," I promised, and marched out in distress, reflecting on the isolation of the lives of station officials in country places. Also on the beguiling—if naïve—way many Indians have of willingly telling you about themselves. Would an English ticket clerk . . .? But the need of bundling the plentiful luggage, tent things and all, into the train interrupted further moralizings.

The little son of the Station Master was dancing about on the platform; at various times of passing by we had made friends. He hung in at my window: "A book? Have you got a book for me this time? I can read well now! "When are you coming again? Please bring me a doll next time you come. My mother says will you come and see her?"

"All right, I will try, next time." If the men suffer from isolation how much more their women? I glanced at the little red-tiled house behind the station, officials' quarters—what lives did its inmates lead? The men have their work, the distraction of trains and the whole railway business (and they know how to make it interesting, too! Many are the tales one hears of the private toll exacted before goods are sent on; my own messengers with my camp goods have not always been exempt). But the women? No goings-on in bazar to watch from the doorstep, no temples near to visit, no neighbours of their caste with whom to have a chat; medical aid far in time of sickness, and the education of sons a problem. Railway communications are an untold boon to India; but I spared a thought of sympathy for those who have to endure some hardship to make them possible.

* * * * *

Of lives in need of sympathy there seem to be many.

I was returning from a village next morning. My way led past a small *tank*.[1] On the *bund*[2] stood the solitary figure of a woman, shading her eyes with her hand and straining to catch sight of something in the distance Her hair and cloth were rudely blown about by the strong monsoon wind.

When she heard my approaching footsteps she turned round towards me, and I saw the tears running down her withered cheeks.

"Oh amma, what is the matter?" I asked in concern.

"My child, my child!" she sobbed. "My only daughter. Look! There she is, going away to her husband's house."

In the distance I could discern some vanishing specks.

"Yes, those are they. How can I go back to my empty house? No one there now, no one to speak to, no one to care for. Oh, my child!"

> ". . . the years, that take the best away,
> Give something in the end;
> And a better friend than love have they,
> For none to mar or mend,
> That have themselves to friend."[3]

"And God as their chief end," I want to add. It may be an impertinence to the poet, but an ultimate truth nevertheless.

Poor lonely Indian mother! How many such have listened wonderingly, in casual encounters such as this, to a message of inner companionship—but what countless more are left uncomforted.

* * * * *

1 Reservoir. 2 Dam. 3 Rupert Brooke.

Later on in the day I sat in the narrow village lane, and to the group that collected related the story of the Prodigal Son. His fate was followed with keen interest. One listener looked up thoughtfully at the end.

"But how shall *we* rise and go to our Father?" she asked.

"Come to my house to-morrow," said another woman. "It is late now, the rice is on the fire, it will spoil if I leave it any longer, but come to-morrow and tell me more. I have never seen a white woman before," she added shyly. "I came to this village when I was married. I was a little girl then. I have never been away since, and not often out of the house. My lord does not like me to go out." In rather dull and drab lives visits by a white woman would rank as an event. "You *will* come?" she urged.

Next morning the sun was not yet over the horizon when Bhagyamma and I were crossing barefoot a wide sandy river, intersected here and there by little runnels of water. As we neared the farther bank and came to a broad shallow sheet of water I saw a motionless woman sitting in the very middle of it. Her face was towards the rising sun, her hands were clasped in prayer; shaven head and red *sari* proclaimed her to be a Brahmin widow. The cleansing water of *Ganga*, the great Mother, softly rippled under and round and, as it were, through her. At that moment the sun leaped over the rim of the earth and smote her full in the face. She bowed once or twice to *Surya Naraina*, the god of the sun, then again remained motionless; her mind was rapt, perhaps her soul too.

The village on the bank was less otherworldly. Near the mosque a glittering spectacle attracted attention; a hawker of silver-ware had laid out his goods, shining bangles, rings, anklets, and necklaces. I took up a thick armlet. "Of what material is this made?" I asked.

"German silver," the vendor rolled out, pronouncing it "Jarrrman." Proudly he presented an English catalogue, printed on cheap paper. Sudra women came crowding round, fingering his goods, asking prices, and starting to bargain. My mind went back to the praying woman seen a few minutes before. Which was the real India? Both, surely. Does not each one of us contain many selves? Then, perhaps, we should ask with which self we are most at home. Which could we permanently endure? And with which of her many selves is India most at home?

I left the chaffering crowd and walked through the village. A little temple stood at the farther end.

"What god is worshipped here?" I asked the passers-by.

"Rama Sami," they answered. They did not seem very friendly.

"And when you have broken coconuts to him . ." I began.

"I don't understand you," interrupted the nearest woman roughly.

". . . does he bless you?" I finished my sentence.

"He does," someone answered curtly. The general temper remained mocking. At this juncture Bhagyamma arrived. I believe the sight of the hawker's wares had detained her. Evidently none of us were in very elevated mood; some distinctly cross even, and the rest in danger of becoming infected. I rallied my forces.

"I spoke to this woman and she says she does not understand me," I began.

"Well, I don't," she broke in again, in the same hostile voice. But a man in the gathering audience seemed to catch the joke.

"But if I said, 'Come, I will give you each a rupee,' would you say you don't understand?" They laughed then, and the ice was broken. In the end they became so friendly that they would not disperse. Someone carried a little paralysed girl to us and begged us to heal her. Ah me, for the power to say, "Rise up and walk!"

We went on to the blacksmith's house. The courtyard was full of peasants waiting for their repair jobs to be attended to. The man works for four villages round, keeping their agricultural instruments in order; in return they give him a share of grain at harvest-time. His mother and widowed sister came out to talk to us; the young wife remained in shy seclusion. He trod the huge bellows, the fire leapt up and a rain of sparks flew; while the irons were heating the women and the peasants listened to our reading and explanation.

"I want to learn to read myself," the young blacksmith called out. "I like your words. Send someone to stay here and teach us."

"We shall forget when you are gone," said a man.

"When it rains a little in the morning it is gone by mid-day," I agreed. "But some grass has been refreshed. The longing for God which is in all your hearts has been strengthened a little, has it not?"

"True," they assented; "but we have a devil, we forget easily."

"Does the smith hammer the iron only once?" I persisted. "Each time we come you will learn a little more."

Outside in the little village-square a banyan and a margosa had been planted close together, the common *Asita Naraina*, signifying married gods. The sight inspired Bhagyamma with a fresh text.

"But how can there be gods without a wife?" a woman broke in. "There are no unmarried gods at all." She became vociferous and even angry in maintaining this argument. The sun had mounted high by now; we were turning riverwards to go back, but a woman plucked me by the arm and bundled me on to her verandah.

"You sit there and teach us wisdom, while I give my son his oil bath," she commanded. The son was a burly young man, presenting to us a bare brown back into which his mother vigorously rubbed oil as she listened. It seemed difficult to get away; on the way to the river we passed some men sitting on a *pial*, and splitting date leaves.

"What is it you teach?" they called out.

Bhagyamma instructed them. "True words," they assented, "but how could we leave our caste?"

"Why are you tearing those leaves?" I asked.

"To make ropes from the fibre," they answered.

"Perhaps caste is like these leaves." I ventured. "As they are now they are no good. They must be split before they can be made into something which will hold. Let us not be afraid to break the outward bond, we may find an inner essence that will be useful."

"Your way is good, but we could never leave our caste," they reiterated.

"Nor will we allow anyone else to leave it," they might have added.

In a village I had planned to reach towards the end of the tour we found ample illustration of this. There two families of the potter caste became Christians some years ago. Since then they have been ceaselessly persecuted. When I reached Mokala they came and sat by the tent for three solid hours, pouring out their woes. And the *Reddi*, the village headman, who should stand for order and fairness, himself led the opposition. The latest ill inflicted was that in Bayana's absence they had taken his wife and beaten her, and now they all felt dishonoured.

"For years we have borne a hundred sorts of trouble. They took away our livelihood by going elsewhere for their pots; we endured hunger; there were many daily ways in which they tormented us. You teach, don't hit back; so they are getting bolder and bolder. They think there is no protection for us; even the catechist was beaten and nothing happened. The teacher was transferred and we are left alone; now this has been done and we have no face left in the village. We are now going to prosecute."

Here were problems. One puzzles and puzzles. Would it be better not to baptize caste families who will have to live in distant villages amid a hostile population, outraged in their sense of loyalty to sacred standards? To break one's caste, what greater sin is there to a Hindu? Is it right to put such a burden of endurance upon these brave and steadfast potter people whose lives are made practically unendurable to them? Or is the Mission to take them out of their surroundings and give them a livelihood by turning them into "Mission agents" though they have no training and are much too old to receive it now?

If anyone has wisdom let them pass it on to us.

"Wait, till you win the community," is the opinion of some missionaries as regards such cases of isolated converts among village artisans. "Don't baptize them and end by turning them into hangers-on in a missionary's verandah, dependent on Western money," is the advice of others, on the same lines. But when I think of the martyrs I am frankly puzzled. If the early Christian Church had never had any? They offended against someone else's loyalty also. Or think of pioneers battling against obscurantism or restriction of liberty anywhere, did it not always mean suffering?

For a day we remained and strengthened and encouraged them as best we could. I believe there is a solution. It does not preclude suffering, but holds at the same time "the way of escape"; whether through inward compensations, or through modification of outward circumstances, is not a matter for dogmatism. But to these people only just emerged from crude village Hinduism, still surrounded by influences driving them to look to the Visible and the Tangible, how make this real?

Moreover, I have a lurking fear that our catechist has a secret joy in litigation—which in general seems to be the pastime of many Indians—and urges the Christians on in that direction. It is a reasonable and just way too. Especially in this case, where one's Anglo-Saxon blood resents the injustice.

* * * * *

By high-ways and by-ways I came to Penuroy town and found myself in entirely different surroundings and atmosphere. Penuroy is a town with a *munsif's*[1] court; hence the presence of many *vakils*. One of them, Mr. V. Sundram Iyer, came to call.

"Would any Brahmin ladies here care for a visit?" I asked him in the course of conversation.

"I will inquire," he said guardedly. Later he returned with a lengthy list of names. "I should let them know when you are coming," he advised.

Doubts arose in my mind. A missionary has not a retinue of *peons*. Here I had but Erana the Faithful. "Do you think I may send my servant? Would they consider it insulting as he does my cooking?" I consulted Mr. Sundram Iyer.

"Please command my services," he said instantly. "I will go myself."

I nearly fell off my chair with amazement. The Brahmin pleader cheerfully to constitute himself a messenger in this matter-of-fact way! I accepted gratefully, and then our talk drifted into matters personal to himself. His wife's education, or rather the lack of it, greatly exercises him. She can read, but does not care about books. He would like intelligent talk with her. Evidently the girl is bewildered, or lazy. Such domestic tragedies when the men have a modern education and the women live in a mental atmosphere many centuries behind, are one of the problems of India. Mr. Sundram Iyer struggles heroically against great

[1] Lower magistrate.

odds; he spoke in a truly delightful way of his mother, whom he taught to read himself after she was widowed and middle-aged. Grandmothers and aunts offered vehement opposition, but he and she persisted, at the cost of domestic peace. Fortunately it did not last. For now regularly every midday the mother gathers other women and reads to them the Vedantas, "so that they shall not spend their time ill." She is greatly respected and receives habitual offerings of fruit and milk; the aged female relatives are now proud of her. O India of many contradictions!

The usual picture of the "poor despised widow" I found similarly out of focus in another Brahmin house. Twenty-five people live in it; there are two or three brothers who are *vakils* and their wives; younger brothers who are still students and *their* wives, also a number of dependent relatives; among the women are four widows. The mistress of the whole household is a widow, the mother of all these sons, a venerable and rather bossy-looking dame. Her head was shaved in orthodox fashion; she wore, of course, not a single jewel, but her *sari* was beautiful. The whole income, hundreds of rupees every month, is given by her sons, the learned *vakils*, to this woman who cannot read, but who rules over that household in all ordinary ways with the power of a complete autocrat.

An equally amazing figure met me in another house. A happy married couple had lived there, Subramanyam Iyer the schoolmaster, a strict Brahmin, but also advanced in his views. He had taught his wife the beginning of reading when in his own middle-age the vision of progress dawned upon him. Other visions must have come to him also, for during an outbreak of plague he worked devotedly in the public interest—then, alas, died of plague himself. His precepts and example lived with Menakshi, his widow; she determined to be his worthy mate. No funeral pyres for live widows now; no useless days and years of mere mourning were to be for her either: he had wished her to study—therefore she, the grey-haired widow, would perfect her reading, she would become a schoolmistress. Consternation, tears, reproaches on the part of female relations in the house, were now her fate; how could she go against the sacred customs? Daily austerities were the duty of the pious Brahmin widow; not this foolish worldly education. Who had ever heard of a high-caste lady wishing to learn it? Besides, who would teach her?

"I can go to the school," she replied steadfastly.

"What? With the little children? Sit on the same bench with ignorant young ones, you the venerable elder?"

Well, it would not be pleasant, Menakshi knew. Inwardly she quaked a little herself, but would not waver from her resolution. Her elder brother then took her part and encouraged her.

So much I had learned from our friend Rangavachari and was eager to see so courageous a pathfinder. I found her busy with a slate, doing with pains and perseverance little sums her brother had set her. She showed me her school books; for she actually goes and sits with the little girls and bears the ridicule. The brave, pioneering spirit! [1]

But the day held a shadow. A Brahmin widow so young that she attracted attention sat among the other women. "What do they call you?" I asked.

"Bimakha."

"How old are you, Bimakha?"

"I am sixteen."

Sixteen and a shaven widow. One meal a day, twice a month a fast day, shut out from all feasts and weddings and joys, and only sixteen. How that poor child must have wept

[1] Note in later years. She succeeded in her enterprise, passed what was then called the primary examination, and underwent normal teacher's training. She is now a greatly respected and beloved mistress in the large Government Girls' School in that town.

when she was shaved and all her wedding finery taken from her!

"Can you read, Bimakha?"

"I have forgotten."

"There is time. Begin again, and you will get on as Menakshi is getting on."

But all have not the heart of a pioneer. Some there are who can carve a way through the rock for themselves, but for the many who need taking by the hand who will win a way?

CHAPTER XIII

IN AND OUT OF THE BOARDING HOME

"And oh, that Sacred Heart burnt up in flame
Against that harsh misleader of our world . . .

* * * * * *

And with one heart-beat of wild ecstasy
I set my heel upon that serpent's head. . . .

* * * * * *

Was't I that did it? Nay the Christ. . . ." [1]

"THAT harsh misleader of our world" makes his presence felt in the little Eden of our Boarding Home.

"Krupi and Shanti have not spoken to each other for three days," reported the Matron. "Other girls are beginning not to be on speaking terms."

Now how to set my heel upon that serpent's head? The two culprits stood before me. I gazed at them in silence.

"Sit down, if you like."

They sat. More silence.

"Are you happy?" I asked at length.

"N-n-no."

Pause. "Are you able to think of any reason why you are not happy?"

"Y-y-yes."

"You are not happy and you know a reason. Now is there anything compelling you to keep on with this reason which is making you unhappy?"

Silence. In the end, "N-n-no; no."

"I see. You are not happy, and you know the reason, and you are not obliged to keep on; but you *do*, since you are not yet happy. I suppose you get something else which you like very much. *What* do you get out of it?"

Silence.

[1] From *The Death of St. Francis*, A. Shearly Cripps.

"Perhaps it makes others happy?" I hazarded.

Silence. "Perhaps it makes a good name for you in the Home?" I went on, very matter of fact. Still no replies.

"Surely you cannot mean that you keep on with what makes neither you nor others happy, for nothing?"

No answer. Perhaps relentless logic was no way with serpents, nor with children.

"Do you know the Lord's Prayer?" I changed the attack. "Very well, say it."

Each girl said it and stopped at a certain petition.

"Why do you stop?" I said casually. "Go on. You, Krupi, say 'As I forgive Shanti here,' and you, Shanti, say 'As I forgive Krupi here'—begin again, and say it right through like that."

Tears, and in the end, a better mind, I hope.

But the old serpent is wily and wriggles away only to reappear.

Some bigger girls came grumbling. "The girls going to the High School won't take their turn in conducting the Christian Endeavour meetings. Will you please tell them to?"

How simple a remedy, to be sure. But what about training willing co-operation in the minds of these cultured damsels, evidently a cut above the others in their own estimation, above the common things like C.E. meetings too.

"Call them here," said the West (perhaps in its turn a shade too ready to rule), and added as a hasty afterthought, "and the girls of the Missionary Committee."

"All arrived. "I have had a brain-wave," said the West brightly, "about our C.E. meetings. Turns are left a little vague now. Should we have a committee that decides them?"

As we have committees about everything, even white ants, this caused no surprise. (The "White Ants Committee," I should explain, has to inspect all the woodwork in the Home daily for the mud-encrusted appearance of these destructive pests, and to paint the preventive solution on.)

"Oh, yes, yes!" they responded eagerly. "Who shall be on it?"

"Would you like to?" This to the High School girls (only four). "And as it is rather an important Committee shall we include the members of the Missionary Committee as well?"

Joyfully the newly constituted members took the oath of fealty.

"It might mean trouble for you," I warned them. "Suppose a girl refuses to take her turn, what would you do?"

Blank puzzledom. "Ask you to tell her to," was all they could think of.

"But that would be saying that you as a committee cannot manage it. You have just promised to do that. If a girl refuses I suppose you would have to punish her. How would you do that?"

"Make her lose her Sunday rosette."

"But that is the Matron's punishment. We cannot interfere with her authority about that."

"Stand her in a corner."

"That is the teacher's punishment in class. Should it not be something that belongs to the Home and to the common life there?"

More plank puzzles. I was driven to suggest gradually, but plainly.

"What about the drama? That is your own thing. If there is a refusal to share in the conduct of the C.E. meeting you can refuse a share in the drama, either as actor or spectator."

Instant chorus: "No! Oh no! No, no!"

"Why not?"

"Because it is such a happy time for everybody."

"Yes, I see that; but is it not true that such a refusal is affecting the happy common life? Has not a girl refusing a common duty forfeited her right to a common pleasure?" I appealed.

"That is true," said Rose. "We will do that."

Rose is the eldest of the High School girls, and the very one who objected to take part. I don't suppose I shall hear any more about refusals, though no necessity to blame or punish anyone has arisen. Certainly make the world safe for democracy!

"Yes, under an oligarchy," does someone say?

"Well, with children," I reply, floored.

We had the drama the next day, and it was a good thing no one was excluded. At Herod's feast a new girl came in as Salome, wearing shorts, and turned the most delicious cartwheels, as light as a feather and as graceful as a fairy. This was a new art in the Home, and afterwards I encouraged the fresh variety-turn. A *palti*! a *palti*! became the general ambition; skirts were tucked up like loin-cloths, the playground grew dusty with cartwheeling girls; some flopped heavily; some tried so hard they were painfully stiff afterwards, and were heartlessly advised to try further practice as a cure, advice heroically followed before their *chota hazri*.

But in big ways and in little, chiefly little, "that harsh deceiver" assaults our world.

The Matron complained of a young teacher being insubordinate to her and stirring up bigger girls with silly and rebellious talk. Things were on the down-grade, evidently; a row had occurred on the way home from school. I had just returned from a long municipal meeting when I heard about this; but there was no time to be tired, only to stand and give battle. Thank God, children are not often hardened sinners; it was pathetic and funny at the same time when three girls came next morning with a written apology, what for they could not say exactly; they had done nothing but listen; they asked pardon "for having no peace in their minds," would I please make them have peace again?

Now God be thanked for this delicate sensitiveness, for this recognition of what is indispensable to them, vague as it is. We traced the evil to consenting to listen to vain and mischievous talk, instead of immediately refusing to lend an ear. They had not grasped the duty of this, only felt uncomfortable, and were touchingly grateful for being shown how to battle and how to be happy again.

With the young teacher the task was harder. "All this trouble has come to me here," she fired off. "Already once you spoke to me very strictly. I never had trouble with Miss Lindsay. No one accused me of anything; here only I am always at fault"—entirely disregarding the fact that it was owing to previous exhibitions of self-will that she had had to be transferred.

Another turned the tables on me even more completely. When I reproved her for using a low word in scolding the children she burst forth vehemently: "Oh, what words I had to swallow when I was in a boarding home; and I fell on the floor before my teachers! But these girls will not even rise when I enter; they are not taught politeness here, and"—finally and crushingly—"if I am so bad how is it that you gave me work as a teacher and allow me to stay in the Home?"

That wily serpent! Well has it taught here the art of converting defence into attack by innuendoes difficult to combat. Even the Matron is not exempt.

Sickness had invaded the Home. I requested a little dysentery patient to show me her tongue. Adhering to it I spied a big grain of raw Bengal gram.

"Where did you get this?" I asked.

"There," pointing vaguely round. From the sick-room I went to the main building. It was the hour of home-work and study. Instead of silence a loud buzz of talk met me.

"What is all this talking?" I said gravely

"I tell them not to," said Matron, who was present and had not stopped it, "but they will do it."

I drew her aside and told her about the Bengal gram.

"Yes, they all do these things. When they grind the raw gram they pick up some and chew it. How many times have I told them not to." She looked at me in the way she has when on self-defence, subtly throwing the blame on me. "That is the kind of Home you have, and those are the kind of girls you bring to it, and with my best endeavours I cannot improve your messes," her look conveys.

Oh ancient cunning!

* * * * *

We struggle on towards perfection nevertheless. "That My joy may be in them" was the girls' verse one Sunday.

"What was His joy?" I asked them.

Stares. "Well, what is your joy?" I prodded.

"To get good marks"; "To go home in the holidays"; To get a letter"; "To pass in the exam"; they chorused.

"Yes, and to put on a pretty *sari*, and to eat sweets, and to have a friend," I eked out the list. "Well now, what was His joy?"

"To save sinners," someone proclaimed piously.

"How is this joy to remain in us?" I pressed. This was too hard to answer. Gradually, at long last, we got round to "doing the will of God." Or I thought we had got there.

"What does doing the will of God mean for us?" I asked hopefully, and far too generally.

Obstinate and conventional piety still held sway. "To turn sinners from their bad ways."

"Oh, and how many sinners did you turn last week?"

"None."

"Then you have not done the will of God and cannot know the joy of Christ?"

Cornered. But it makes one sigh to see "the harsh deceiver" masquerading as an angel of light, in the superficial phrases too often used by "Mission agents" in a lazy, shallow way, catching the very elect, these dear children sitting here and looking at me with perplexed eyes. Well, start again.

"Let's take to-day. You got up, and then . . . ?"

"Prayers." They were still hopelessly pious.

"No, not at once."

"We washed first."

"Is there any will of God about that?"

Stares. My innings at last. Bodies—temples of God; presumably He likes them clean—and so straight on about all daily details; a will of God about each, and therefore the chance of Christ's joy open to us all. Their shining responsive faces revealed how easily and naturally they live in the kingdom which—in what was surely one of His most daring sayings—Christ declared to be theirs.

But they are not saved from having to think for themselves.

"Is there a hell?" they asked me conversationally when we were out together for our Sunday afternoon walk. "The catechist at Ramidi said there was not. He said if a person did wrong would his father burn him and punish him to bring him to a good mind?"

"Do *you* know anything about hell?" I countered.

They looked at me wonderingly.

"Have you ever done anything wrong? And tried to hide it? You have? How did you feel? What you felt then was of the nature of hell."

Silence followed. This had to be digested. I walked on in the dusty evening with the gleam of sunset in the hot grey sky.

A little hand stole into mine. Jewel was looking up at me anxiously.

"If you got to the other side and were sorry could you be received?"

The others pressed forward to hear the reply; a little fear and suspense in their faces. I had not denied the possibility of hell as blithely as the catechist.

"Could you be received?" urged Jewel.

"What do you think? If a girl had been horrid to you and were sorry would *you* receive her?"

Jewel looked reassured. Well she might; the springs of love in her little heart do not fail. But it is incredibly hard for us all to learn that God is at least as kind as we are. As for infinite Love—the words are incomprehensible.

Excited babble arose behind me. The children were discussing the mighty theme. I left them to form their own theology. Had the serpent's head—doubting God—been scotched?

* * * * *

Its live and actual namesake troubles us much here. These encounters do not grow stale with repetition. And as about twenty thousand people die in India every year of snake bites we have reason for our excitements. I was making biscuits in the dining-room at midday when a snake glided in at the open verandah door. I saw it coil itself under the couch, and hastily went for a cane. But by the time I returned it had disappeared. Gone out again, disturbed by my steps, I surmised. When I returned in the evening from bazar I found an excited scene; Flower's quick eyes had seen a snake glide into the room, there it was again under the couch. Servants were busy lighting lanterns.

"Put a saucer with milk near and wait for it to come out," advised a visitor arriving at that precise moment. No such performance of *naga-puja* (snake worship) for us! We moved the couch, the snake slid under the bamboo matting. I have had this happen before, in another house, and never caught that creature; the experience of expecting to feel a live snake squelch under your tread I had no desire to repeat;

we lifted the mat. If it were a cobra it could not strike until it reared, as cobras can only strike horizontally, though they do this with lightning quickness. The career of this one was, however, ended before it had the chance; a full-grown cobra it turned out to be, eight feet long.

We were not so lucky in our next snake hunting; a midnight adventure in the Boarding Home. Some sixth sense—or a guardian angel?—awoke the matron, who saw, to her horror, a large cobra in the farther end of the room where no one was lying, but no break in the floor space divided the sleepers from the reptile, which was in full battle array, head erect, hood extended, hissing loudly. Another shape also was moving about, but she did not stop to examine, only shook the nearest girl awake. The cry "snake!" had a very immediate effect; each big girl seized a still slumbering little one, and in no time they were all out in the courtyard safely, the door bolted upon the snake inside, still loudly angry. When lanterns were lifted at windows they saw the snake was fighting with a great bandicoot, a creature of the rat tribe. That the bandicoot had got in a touch was evident by the serpentine line of gory marks on the floor, exhibited to my thrilled eyes next morning; but the finish *à outrance* took place beyond human eyes; the snake slid between the floor slabs where mortar had crumbled away and disappeared, the bandicoot after it, and that was the end of the circus for the night. Next morning we got an iron bar; the waterman showed considerable reluctance to lever up the first slab; "it went under there," warned the matron. So I raised it myself, expecting to hear the cobra's hiss, but nothing followed, though slab after slab was taken up. We found the bandicoot's passage, which we closed, but no corpses. A bandicoot can bite its way through masonry even, a snake has no such facilities; so we hoped it was safely interred and proceeded to refix our slabs, with cement this time!

The girls were very brave about it; indeed, they learn to

be ready for emergencies themselves. I had just stepped out of the Home one evening, and was distant but a few yards from the door, when the dreaded call rang out, "snake!" Before I had regained the door I heard the reassuring, "Kesha has killed it."

"Good girl," I praised warmly, for the quick mental work as well as grit; she could not have lost a fraction of a second in rushing for a stick and applying it.

Yet, suddenly, the girls are subject to "herd psychology" in freakish ways. Every day samples of their food are brought to me; but instead of two children eagerly looking to see me choke over the hot curry—a pleasure that never palls—matron herself appeared one night. "Sundari and Dana came running back, saying they had seen some black shapes near the well, now no girl will go out."

"Silly geese," was the comment; "let them have their suppers and go to bed."

Next night I was there at dusk. "I hear some of you were frightened yesterday. Is anyone willing to run to the end of the playground alone?"

"I!" "I!" "I will!" One of the smallest children was dispatched.

"I will run alone right round the Home and playground outside the wall!" volunteered Margaret, a little scornfully.

"Taken—go!" There is only a lonely wilderness behind the Home.

"Will anyone run alone to the bungalow?"

Another courageous atom departed, though the way lay past the well. The dusk was condensing, however, and the fear of snakes too real to make this experiment safe any longer.

"Is anyone willing to stay ten minutes alone in the dark sick-room?"

The nervous girl who had started the trouble volunteered for solitary confinement.

"Anyone for the dark store-room?"

Her fellow-sinner was shut up. Then a whispered conspiracy took place. Three or four were chosen to make a sudden noise of terror outside the two doors closed upon the prisoners. This they did with gusto; but perhaps it was too artificial, or all were keyed to heroic pitch; no answering shriek came from inside. They were let out; as I followed everybody into the main hall I envisaged a frightful thing beyond the opposite door opening into black darkness and let out a scream of fear; the dark corners behind the archways also held for me horrible shapes, causing gasps of terror. But all conceit of acting was taken out of me; from the first the children only shouted with laughter; grimace I never so gruesome, the teachers rocked with delight, even the matron held her sides, while the children yelled for joy: the ghosts of fear, however, retired beyond the precincts, routed. There are various ways of setting your heel upon serpents.

But the adversary has ways of getting back a little of his own; if not in inner ways then in outward—and not only snakes are a trouble here. We had been having school inspection all the morning, so the afternoon was a holiday. All of us gaily set out for a walk whithersoever the children would They elected to visit a teacher's new baby in the Extension, about one and a half miles away. In the courtyard of the house a rather restless cow was tied up; I slid by hastily when I saw her manifest strongly anti-British tendencies, and disappeared into the room. When we had all taken our turn in admiring the baby and it became time to leave I looked for a back exit, to save the cow's feelings; but as there was none I asked the teacher's mother, who owned the animal, to stand by and keep it calm. She talked to it soothingly and I, thinking all safe, made for the gate. What happened then happened too quickly for detailed impression on my brain; the creature must have gone *berserk*, wrenched out the peg it was tied to and made straight for me—for my next memory is the feeling of the cow's horns in my hands as I wrestled with it, and then the sight of my skirt, covered with gore. I had also a mental flashlight of a scene witnessed two weeks before when the children and I happened to be in hospital and saw a girl carried in who had been gored by a buffalo; she had died the next day. Something else must have acted in my brain, besides memory, I found myself back in the room and there saw that my left wrist was streaming. The children began to scream, naturally, and indeed I was a horrid spectacle. Jewel retained her wits; when I said "water," she brought it in a trice, though in a narrow vessel; then recognized in a flash something shallow was needed and got a brass plate. While bathing my wrist I tried to quiet the others, loudly lamenting. The cow had made for freedom; the girls waiting outside fled shrieking, all but Margaret, whom an earthquake would not move out of her wits; she calmly turned the creature into a neighbouring yard, where it was securely fastened. The teacher tied up my bleeding left wrist; the right wrist and fore-arm were badly bruised and sprained—there must have been *some* tussle with that cow! The nerves of the arm were making such a din that I did not hear another murmur, though I thought there might be a bruise on the body. I sent for a *jatka* to take me home, but none could be found; so, after a rest, I set out, two girls keeping faithful hands in the broad of my back, pushing me forward, else I could never have walked the distance, for an exhaustion was upon me.

When we reached home at last an agitated compound met us; shrieks of dismay had to be soothed; I rather longed for someone to take charge of everybody, myself included. Dorcas, on hearing of the accident, had fled to its scene, unfortunately by a different route, so we had missed her. I got upstairs at last, and then discovered a gashly abdominal wound which had been bleeding like a pig all the way (I had attributed the gore on the skirt to the wrist slash). A nice mess I was in! My right hand was useless with pain, the left with the bandaged wrist not in good case, but I got out of my clothes at last, and in the end Dorcas returned, and sponged and bandaged. The doctor was sent for; alack! he had just left for camp. I held a pad on the wound all night, as the bandage slipped at once, and I could not sleep in any case; one might call it not a very good night. But it passed. Our new assistant lady surgeon came next morning, a charming Indian girl, but a bit timid still about her work; this was her first post. She was so scared at the gash (about five inches long) that she said the D.M.O. (district medical officer) must see it, though I begged her to stitch it up. However, she bandaged it, which was a relief. Not till the following day did the doctor return, who shook his head and said it should have been treated earlier, now it would have to be burnt (my visions of red-hot pokers were relieved by the sight of iodine!); also stitches were not likely to hold after this lapse of time. But they did, nor were his fears of things going septic realized. The wound healed with remarkable celerity, while I led the lazy life of luxury and ease so often yearned for; Jewel and Flower to fetch and carry, Margaret to massage the arm; she turned out to have the most extraordinary *flair* for doing it just right, and will have to be trained for something medical.[1] So what with this discovery, and a rest cure, and undeserved sympathy pouring in—for the story, gloriously exaggerated, spread about everywhere—we seem to have got more out of it than the adversary, after all.

* * * * *

And so back to normal life. Prize-givings generally follow on the heel of inspections, but the undisciplined cow had caused a delay. The event, however, was reached in the end;

[1] She is in training as a nurse at the time of writing.

my study was crowded in every corner with messes, dolls, parcels, lists, labels, prizes of all sorts—also girls. Strange how many needs they had that day; or if their powers of discovering reasonable requests failed, there were peepings and pointings and whispers at the window, followed by shameless, because reasonless, entrances, met by me Jove fashion, with thunders freely strewn round. Apparently that only served to stimulate invention, fresh ideas were born, a smiling little face, a polite voice: "*Namaskaram*! will you please . . ."

"I won't!" I roared. "I won't have you here, or your *namaskaram*. I only want 'Go!' "

Giggles and whispers in the verandah, delighted repetition: "I don't want *namaskaram*! I won't have you here. I only want 'Go!' "

Unfortunately just then the pastor came in, with his three little sons; "they can weed in your garden while we talk," he suggested. They did, or pretended to, and then considered themselves entitled to roam my room at will while their father went on to other houses in the compound. The verandah-ites took heart of grace and crept in again and hid under chairs, while I was expected to go sniffing round, "Fi fo fum, I smell children!" accentuated by awful thrills, "I smell a little girl! I smell a fat little boy!" followed by ill-suppressed sighs of bliss under the furniture. But the wise little people always instantly recognize the change of voice when it remarks casually, but finally, "now it's enough, run home"; and trot off without fuss.

* * * * *

In matters religious we try to follow the same happy naturalness; I of the sophisticated West, feel at times fearful of bringing up little prigs; yet directness and simplicity must surely be right if the blessedness which the unique vision of Christ saw belonging to children is to be real to them.

A missionary sick with headache dismissed the little juniors after a very short Sunday lesson. "Prayer?" they said wonderingly.

"Not to-day," they were told, and began to troop out. But five or six lingered.

"There are some girls sick," they pleaded; "may we not pray for them?"

"Of course," was the reply; so they knelt down and each put up her little sentence of petition that they might be healed. "May the medicine they take be heavenly medicine," asked one. Others came back to see why these lingered, and seeing what was to the fore knelt down too and added their mites. All with a simple seriousness that was lovely to see. It made one realize one's blessings in the Mission field Here, in these country stations, we are not yet confronted with a sophisticated generation.

* * * * *

The *dhobi* came with a long face. Two miles away by the river where he had taken our girls' clothes—eighty-nine articles—five thieves came, tied him up and ran off with all the eighty-nine. A loss of about two hundred rupees to us; how it is to be made good no one can guess.

Chits were sent off to the police. Consternation tended to reign in the Home. The parents are all poor, and cannot repeat the already great effort of a girl's outfit; yet it is not fit that the children go ragged and dirty. It happened that Elijah was our lesson on Sunday, book and raven and cruse of oil. I asked them if the same God was still alive? If He could do the same things? If there were any promises anywhere about clothes? Though the big ones could quote Matthew vi. 28–30, they seemed afraid to; it was all right, evidently, to trust God to give you clothes when you had them already; but when they had been stolen how could He? I felt not unlike this myself, yet spurred myself to read aloud the words: '*Shall He not much more clothe you, O you* girls and teachers *of little faith*, in the Andapur Boarding Home?"

Little Murti, a new-comer, who finds her way to my study on every excuse she can think of, drank it in and presented her petition in the chain-prayer with fine directness. "Please, Father, the clothes have gone; give us some, Amen."

Later on about two-thirds of them were recovered by the efforts of the police, and a special gift helped to re-buy the best part of the remainder. Murti took it as a matter of course. Some of the older ones said with shining faces, "Didn't we ask God every day? Now it has come right."

CHAPTER XIV

GREYING GOLD

Is India's old order passing? Sometimes my mind misgives me. There are signs of coming changes. Incidents occur, articles are written in the Press and in magazines, which indicate increasing irreligiousness in the rising generation, as well as growing political unrest.

This last may at times be actually felt even in our quiet Andapur, though the reason for agitation may not be grasped very well. At breakfast one day Rama Dao announced with a grin that he had got some mutton in spite of all shops being shut.

"Oh, they are keeping *hartal*, then?" I remarked.

"It is a Government order," explained Rama Dao.

"You mean Mr. Gandhi's order," I corrected.

"Oh yes, yes. The Prince is passing, they are making it a holiday for everybody."

That was the lucid conception of Non-Co-operation which bazar gossip contained and conveyed.

Later in the day the Christian head mistress came with her report. Our school had been held as usual as the Prince's passing was strictly private. All had gone quietly, children came as on other days, but in the late afternoon an invasion of zealous young Non-Co-operators occurred. Without asking anybody's permission they burst into the school. "Don't you know it is *hartal*? How dare you keep school?"

The head mistress is of small stature, but she boldly faced her compatriots.

"This is a girls' school, there are only women here; how dare you come in?"

"Will you close, or will you not?" they returned roughly.

"If you will all go out we shall close presently," she said

pacifically. It was within half an hour of closing time then; by shortening the regular time by only a quarter of an hour honour was preserved; both sides came off with flying colours.

Otherwise, few reverberations reach us here. Though who can tell what is going on under the surface?

Even from our little country town young men now find their way to England. A woman of the merchant caste came up to ask me for news of her son, gone to Europe. She was quite illiterate herself; she also had the idea that all white people knew one another and that I could easily find out from "my people" why he did not write. In the end, through a mutual friend, information was obtained; later on the young man returned with brilliant degrees. And with much else. He was now a burning Swarajist; his torrent of fiery speech and indignation revealed an inner volcano before which arguments were futile. Also he was now completely irreligious. In the quiet of my study his lava-like stream of words was innocuous; but elsewhere? He was paying only a brief visit to his home, being on the way to his new post, a Government one. Logic I have rarely found to be a powerful factor in Indian minds.

His old mother still has images of Sarasvati and Ganpati on the sacred shelf in her kitchen and faithfully performs her daily worship before them; does her pride in his achievements—which she does not understand—outweigh her grief at his having cast off all ways of piety? The bitterness of clash between the old and the new must inevitably become more accentuated as Indian history moves on. Or is there a way out?

Round about here it is still the old religious India; one still meets the old quick response.

It was Sunday morning, a municipal *peon* arrived with notices, demanding signatures.

"I will take them this time," I said, "so as not to give you extra trouble, but do not come again on Sunday. We must keep one day separate for Divine things."

The man looked up with quick understanding. "Yes, that is true. We forget about God. So we have not His blessing."

As good a sermon as I heard presently in church. His reply was not, I felt sure, dictated by mere politeness. Perhaps ancient tax-gatherers with secret religious longings still have their modern counterparts in India.

One meets signs along roadsides, or on station platforms, or anywhere.

I was walking across the fields to the station at Dharmpalli and passed a quarry. *Woddars* (stone-breakers) were at work in it. They stopped to gaze, and I to greet, then heard their tale of woe, the usual one. Firewood was so dear; it cost three times as much now to split rocks, how were they to live? [1]

I have no magic wand to wave away the ills of our life; a bit of secret bread was all that could be offered. "God gives us each our own burdens, also He helps us to bear them."

Remembering that trains will not wait for sermons I went on and heard behind me: "This is a lucky day. The Messengers have visited us to-day." There is the atmosphere; India's immediate appreciation of a word, however brief, of spiritual matters. Will modern political and economic stirrings destroy it? Will mills and factories and encroaching industrialism kill that simple homage to the Unseen, vague and undeveloped as it often is?

When I reached the road I saw a man stoop repeatedly and strew something on the ground from a paper bag. "What are you doing?" I asked him. Questions by strangers and wayside talk are taken as a matter of course in this friendly country.

"I am giving sugar to the ants."

[1] The usual method of quarrying is to heat the rock or boulder by burning wood piled up against it, and splitting while hot.

Ah, yes—to gain merit. To have an offset to *Karma* and the weight of accumulated sin.

"God will think kindly of your kindly thought, I doubt not," I said, hurrying on.

I need not have been in such haste. The train was two hours late. I settled on the platform under a shady tree, with my writing-case. A Brahmin widow strolled up. "A gift, please."

I bestowed a small coin and earned small merit. Talk followed. The woman's straight and sincere gaze was attractive. I felt certain she pursued ideals; the quest could be seen in her earnest eyes, even before I learned that she was a pilgrim from one holy place to another. One of India's innumerable seekers; throughout the ages, from Kashmir to Travancore, there has never failed a succession of Indian men and women who have put the needs of the soul before those of the body, faring hopefully along far roads, to sacred rivers and distant temples, looking for redemption.

> "Friends and loves we have none, nor wealth nor blest abode,
> But the hope of the City of God at the other end of the road.
>
> * * * * * *
>
> We travel from dawn to dusk, till the day is past and by,
> Seeking the Holy City beyond the rim of the sky.
>
> Friends and loves we have none, nor wealth, nor blest abode,
> But the hope of the City of God at the other end of the road." [1]

Para-deshi (from the Sanscrit *para* = other; i.e. other-worldly, or heavenly; *desh* = country; *deshi* = one of that country) is one of their words for "pilgrim"; does it not *declare plainly that they seek a country*?

Beloved soul of India, rooted more deeply than that of other races in the Unseen!

Of common castes the pilgrims were often, even beggars some of them, revered nevertheless by all. A few won

[1] Masefield, *The Seekers.*

renown by their poetic gifts, as well as by their saintliness; their songs are still household treasures.

My chance acquaintance would not ever be of that last high company; her respect for words was too scanty; she spilled them forth heedlessly in the manner of the garrulous; my chief contribution was, perforce, silent listening. But the presence or the absence of words is never the main thing, surely; below the speech or the silence communication of another kind took place,—who can explain these things? Something was dear to the soul of this traveller that was dear to mine also; we each recognized it. The Indian woman tried to put it into words, always a risky thing, especially with Oriental floweriness.

"I knew you were a great one; when I saw you sitting there I said, here is a great one," she confided as she followed me to the train, which had come in at last. Thus will one *para-deshi* ever recognize another.

"Do not wait here in the blazing sun," I begged her as she stood by the compartment; "go back to the shade of the tree."

"When it rains we take water," she responded calmly. "I shall not see you again; but this has been a day of joy to me."

No less to me. A sudden awareness of spiritual sympathy is ever as a draught of living water. She had not given me any chance to speak of experiences on my own pilgrim way, but sometimes silence may prepare the way of the Lord. She accepted some Gospels and Psalms. "I will keep them always, always," was her farewell as the train steamed out. Perhaps their study will yet bring her pilgrimage to an unexpected and satisfying goal.

But what a country, where common workmen and wayfarers, meeting signs of spiritual pursuits, or messages, immediately call them great! And what a basis in this receptive atmosphere for our message! An atmosphere surely affecting all, of whatever creed.

My Mohammedan teacher came up at night. We sat in the moonlit garden while she poured out her story. She had had a great deal of bother about land and law and relations and suits while away on leave; these had to be explained. But when I began to wonder if requests for help were to follow she suddenly changed into another key.

"Do you remember talking one day about believing in God and letting Him manage our lives, doing our best and then accepting what He sent and not feeling anxious? That came home to me. I followed that way and believed. I left off worrying. And now look what has happened."

Apparently things had gone remarkably smoothly, and help had come in a way that astonished her. "Not one word has failed!"

"Will you remember that when the next trouble comes?" I asked.

"I will, I will!" she said joyously, not yet realizing, perhaps, how long and hard is the fight of faith.

My thoughts went off to the evangelistic field our non-Christian teachers present. Many a missionary school, High school, and college could give moving examples of Indian response to Christian atmosphere, in teachers perhaps even more than in scholars. Whatever they may remain outwardly the association tells. Moti Bi and I have been working together for ten years. Now at the end of them she is learning to believe in God. That is as far as we have got. And then, at this very time, there is an agitation from our Home Board to turn out all non-Christian teachers from our schools *en bloc.* Is it all to the good? Sometimes I think there is no more splendid opportunity than our fellow-teachers.

But even casual contact reveals prepared ground.

I was sitting in the bazar among a group of women, telling them the story of Daniel in the lions' den. I had just come out of school, where the children had been acting it, and nothing else was in my mind. Or was I getting into the same mental state as some of our teachers? The stories beloved of them, and ever retold, are: Jonah and the whale, Daniel and the lions, Elisha and Naaman (indeed, I found this so firmly fixed in one teacher's mind that a New Testament leper had the same instructions given to him as Naaman), and the rich man and Lazarus. All these offered great chances of lurid description. Certainly much excitement prevailed in my audience.

"So he was thrown in."

A groan went round. "Alas, alas!" "Finished, finished!"

"No, not finished," I resumed. Renewed attention.

"But what *bhakti*!" "Where have *we* got such devotion?" exclaimed the listeners at the end.

"And there are lions about here, too," I went on.

"Where, where?"

"There is one"—pointing to the toddy[1] shop.

"Yes, it is a lion, that is true," said several women. But another sat silent and thoughtful. Presently she looked up. "Are there any other lions?" she asked earnestly.

Ah, that eager look of the dumb soul, momentarily awake and aware of the Divine Spirit in the depth of being; seeking to draw them to God! That question implied longing and a sense of need; she wanted something to supply it, the toddy temptation was none of hers; but there were others. There it was, the prepared ground.

And then one comes on the thorns and weeds of their mistaken fears.

As I was leaving a woman was seized with, I think, an attack of asthma; she fought so for breath.

"The ghost of her husband has seized her!" cried the quickly increasing crowd. The husband had died two months ago.

Vainly I tried to dispel the notion. "Make her better, heal her!" they cried then. "You can, you know about *bhakti*;

[1] Countrymade liquor.

there, take her hand, heal her!" the women pleaded. The patient was already in the open; I could only make people stand off, then fan her, and talk soothingly, telling her it would pass; she showed signs of losing self-control. Presently she calmed down and after a long while grew a little easier. With pity one thinks of what future attacks may mean for the poor sufferer; for relations often resort to methods amounting to cruelty to drive out the ghost. In that and similar respects one longs for the old to pass away in India!

There are, however, human frames of mind which will always remain. In demands made of God they are very like ourselves.

An old woman sat in the door of her hut, listening. Her face was furrowed with lines of grief.

"Yes, I believe your words; I, too, was serving God. But I said God must keep my last son alive, my husband had gone, and all others; the remaining one must live, I said. But he, too, died. Why, oh why did God let my son die before he had a son? Now there is always burning in my heart. I cannot talk to God, or think of Him, or serve Him. If He had kept my son alive I would have."

They shall be comforted. Those that weep, it says; bitter human tears are enough. From that vast Pity even the bargain-makers are not excluded. Well He knows it is only because they do not understand.

"It is her *Karma*," said the others; "she has a bad *Karma*."

I launched forth into the story of the two debtors. Another grey-haired woman pressed near, listening with concentrated attention.

"Do you mean to say God would just forgive?" she interrupted, doubt in her voice.

I paused, taken aback by the greatness of the question.

"We go in the road, we think, we speak, we work in the house," she went on, "and it all has sin; sin is mixed up with all we do. And you say,—do you really mean to say,—God will forgive simply when we ask?"

It seemed to me as if the soul of India, with its despairing doctrine of *Karma*, were looking from the sad eyes of the questioner. "Will He just forgive?"

No, not "just," or "simply."

> ". . . . 'tis by no breath,
> Turn of eye, wave of hand, that salvation joins issue with death."

The meeting-place of the sin of the world and the Love of God could not but be one of a battle beyond our imagination. To counteract, to neutralize, the terrific potency of men's accumulated wrong choices—what overwhelming forces of love and sacrifice have to become operative? The human heart cannot easily believe that story. O wise and wonderful Lord Christ! He knew that all of us have to learn Divine Forgiveness in possible human ways. "If ye forgive men their trespasses . . ."

This woman's heart was not weighed down, I think, by the burden of some special sin. The mountainous load of the law of *Karma* oppressed her; unconscious sin, as well as conscious, relentlessly causing future evil results. A logical philosophy India possesses in this doctrine, containing a deep truth; but a ray of hope, a light for the daily path of struggling men and women, no. Here was one poor, oppressed heart, bowed under the weight of *Karma*; one thinks of the innumerable ones like her, to whom is owed the unique message of a Divine Love revealed by a Cross as well as by a Life.

* * * * *

Here and there we come upon signs that He has passed by. I was sitting in a village home, among a group of women. A bangle-seller strolled in at the open door and joined the crowd. In the stir caused by her depositing her glittering wares I paused in my talk and noticed a big scar on the newcomer's forehead.

"Have you had a burn?" I asked her.

"No, it was a tumour. I nearly died. I had to go to Madras."

"Who treated you?"

"A white Missiamma like you."

"How much did you pay her?"

"Nothing. She did not ask me. I am poor, I could not earn anything during that month."

"Why did you not go to your own people's hospital?"

"Ram, Ram, do the brown people have hospitals?" She laughed derisively. "You Christian people[1] do; much merit is yours."

"Then do you understand what your scar signifies?" I asked again.

No one did. "Christ's writing on the forehead," I said. The audience became still, for writing on the forehead is portentous. The phrase refers to the lines in the skull made by the bones fitting together. According to Hindu ideas they are written by Brahma and indicate a person's fate. The curious wording of the phrase seemed to make it legitimate to point to the scar and interpret it as I did. "The marks of His love, inspiring a follower of His to imitate His work of healing," I explained.

"We shall remember Him now," said the woman, "when we see the scar."

"Thus is He writing on the face of India," I wound up, "a helping, a healing, if India will let Him." But even while we were thinking of such possibilities daily life took us in its grip again.

[1] I can but record what she said. There are hospitals and refuges now, built and maintained by "brown people." But she may have felt instinctively that Hinduism did not contain within it the driving power to make such efforts for others, but that another religion did.

The doorway darkened afresh, coolie women who had worked all day in fields belonging to this household pressed in with their load of garnered cotton. The mistress of the house came forward and the wage distribution began. Each coolie tipped out her basket on the floor, the mistress divided the contents in half. One half she made into eight parts, of which the coolie chose one. That was her wage, one-sixteenth of her own picking. In an eight-hour day seven and a half hours would be for her employer's benefit and half an hour for her own. It seemed rather sweated labour.

"How long does it take to collect enough cotton for a cloth for yourself?" I asked.

"One month."

And then it has to be cleaned of seeds, and spun, woven and dyed. But they were very cheerful over it. It is not the poor who are the worst off in this life of ours.

Unless they are too hardly pressed. With us monsoons fail frequently and times of scarcity recur often. The Boarding Home girls came with tales of famine in the villages; people were eating aloe-roots and the like. Evidence of want came home to ourselves, not only in high prices. Thieves climbed several times over the wall, searching in the courtyard of the Home for leavings. Once they found a tumbler, nothing the next time; so they carried off the two heavy grinding-stones, four weighty halves. They must have been hunger-driven indeed to go off with such a burden which they could only sell secretly and cheaply.

Then one fine morning Obi Reddi, the father of two girls in the Home, stood in the verandah—had he come to ask to get their fees remitted? No, worse, he pushed a little girl forward: "take her, teach her. I paid her fare. I cannot see her starve. Her people have nothing." (I could hear Committee reminding me of rules and of our financial limitations!) "I put that bit of cloth on her," Obi Reddi went on urging. "I can't do more; we are at an end ourselves"

"All right, she can stay this month," I said feebly; "perhaps there will be rain, then her people will earn and can pay fees."

"How long before the harvest," replied Obi Reddi, "even if rain comes now? *We* are going to Assam."

I knew the "coolie catcher" had been round; trying to persuade village labour, idle here, to move to a far country,—a new thing in these parts.

One reads the portent. New conditions are ushering in a new order. And in as far as it means that during famines people will not die in shoals, as formerly, one cannot be too thankful for changes; it is all to the good that during scarcity (i.e. not yet the complete terror of famine) villagers can go and find work in more fortunate climes, or in mills and mines and factories. It is also urged that when they return—for they nearly always do return; the Indian villager loves his home and few settle at a distance—their horizon is widened, their outlook enlarged. Without doubt. But enlarged in what way? That is where fears for the coming days sometimes overtake me.

What will be the effect of the impact of the commercial and industrial spirit on the rural India of the future? Will contact with "civilization" destroy that simple homage to the Unseen, and the supremacy granted so readily now to spiritual values by ordinary people, however filled with anxiety for daily bread their poverty may cause them to be? Change is the law of life; India cannot escape it; but need it be a change involving incalculable losses? What efforts ought not to be put forth now to help her to preserve—and to possess in greater completeness—her heritage of belief in the fundamental spirituality of life? The assailants to this faith are increasing in her own midst; misgivings cloud the outlook. Will tax collectors of the future no longer respond to an admonition to remember God, or worldly-minded teachers struggle to learn trust in Him; or women, conscious of sin and *Karma*, ask questions about forgiveness; or pilgrims go on their quest for peace and deliverance? That the *Atma*, the Spirit, and not the body or anything material, is the true Reality, is still India's conviction. But will it wane, as the consequence of the irreligious education received by so many of her sons?

"*Paramatma!*"—Spirit other than I, yet also within—has been her fervent prayer through the ages, and thus many still pray. And we with them. "*Paramatma!*" It is a name of God at once so comprehensive and so intimate that in some moods I find it slipping into my private prayer. "*Paramatma!* Let not India lose her fight of faith in Thee, but win through to that true knowledge of Thyself and of Him whom Thou hast sent, which is Life eternal."

CHAPTER XV

FERVENT IN SPIRIT

The little sunbaked mud huts of the village stood silent in the heat of noon. The workers in the fields around and the women at home were all enjoying a midday sleep in the hot, drowsy air; no one was stirring.

Slowly the door of a hut opened; a woman looked out cautiously, then turned and beckoned to someone behind.

"This is the time," she said, "no one is about. Take the rope."

A younger woman came out and looked doubtfully at her.

"Do you really mean it, sister? I feel afraid." Nervously she twisted the well-rope in her hand.

"Yes, come," said the elder one with determination. "What good can life bring to us poor widows? Only dishonour. Do you know one single widow in our village who could hold on to righteousness? There is no comfort anywhere. Oh, how many pilgrimages have I gone! No god has answered me. I cannot bear the thought of the long years ahead. I am going to end it."

"I am afraid," said the younger sister again. "Must I come?"

"It would be sin to leave you behind alone, little sister," said the elder tenderly. "Come! It will soon be over."

Together they went out of the village. A woman stirring from her sleep on the verandah looked after them. "Widow Lakshmi and her sister," she muttered; "where are they going? With a rope and no pots? They are bereft of sense."

The sisters had passed through the village to the fields. Deserted and quiet in the midst of the *ragi* cultivation was the large square well used for its irrigation on alternate days. To-day was an off day and no one was near. The sisters went down the rough steps and stood by the water. The elder took the rope and twisted it round them both. Round them rose the strongly revetted walls of the well; above them hung the little stone platform whence, on other days, the great leather bag would be let down over the simple hasp to bring up the precious liquid from the cool depths to the thirsty fields.

The younger girl stared fearfully at the dark water.

"Come, sister," said the elder one, "let us jump in. We will leave this world of illusion together. Now!" Resolutely she stepped to the very edge.

But the younger one gave a cry of horror. "No, no, *no*, I will not! Not into that black water! I can't do it, sister, I don't want to die!"

In terror lest she should be dragged in she slipped an arm out of the rope, threw the rest over her head and scrambled as fast as her trembling limbs would allow up the steps, and ran back home.

"My poor little sister," thought the elder, "she has no strength. Shall I go by myself? But it would be much sin to me if I left her, without any near relative in the world. I, too, must stay."

Mournfully she went home.

* * * * *

It was in a tent at midday that the sisters told me of this dark day in their past which had so nearly brought two lives —now happy and useful—to the despairing step, taken by so many Hindu widows, of suicide. Many years of searching after God had followed, the story of which is told elsewhere.[1] India holds many unsatisfied hearts, strenuous and unwearied in their search for God; the elder of these two was such a one. Not a few pilgrimages to sacred shrines and holy rivers had she made—in vain; no priestly blessing, or acceptance of her offerings—no bathing in holy waters or shaving her

[1] *A Struggle for a Soul*, Chap. A Seeker. R.T.S.

head at Tirupati or Kadiri—no sacrifice of her savings and jewels to temples—not the trudging of weary miles or the learning and chanting of endless verses, could quench her thirst. But when at length, in response to a strange inner command, she set out for Bukkuru, a place which was not at all an object of pilgrimage generally, she met some Christians and heard from them the story of Jesus Christ. Her long quest was ended; the craved-for deliverance from fear and inward bondage was found.

What a disciple she became, putting to shame many of us to whom the priceless knowledge so eagerly sought by her is offered at less cost. After some instruction at Andapur she desired to work at Bukkuru, the town where she had first heard of Christ. Her enthusiasm was as a mountain torrent, carrying others with her wherever she lived. Caste prejudices towered round her; engrossment in daily affairs and the indifference to spiritual things which so easily beset us all threatened to silt up the clear water, but her simplicity found practical ways out.

"Come and pray with me," she would say at sundown to neighbouring women, who had often laboured in the fields themselves, or else done the cooking and house-work for those who went out. Nightly a little circle gathered round her; they learned to join in the lyrics she sang to them; her direct and simple prayers invited imitation; in any case she expected it of them.

"You pray now, Nallamma," she would demand.

"It does not come to me," replied Nallamma timidly.

"Ask God to bless you and forgive your sins," Radha would exhort. And if a hearer were still diffident: "Well, say it after me, then," she would uphold the weak. And so, some courageously swimming, some helped by the plank of docile repetitions, all came to that desirable shore of learning for themselves direct speech with the Unseen.

"If only you would read for yourselves too," she would

hammer the heating iron, "how much you could learn at other times!"

"Reading does not come to us," they objected.

"Did it come to me?" she said undiscouraged. "Are there not silver threads in my hair? Yours is still black. You can learn what I learnt."

Here and there a woman began. Some persevered. Not a few women owe to her their capacity for reading the Gospels for themselves. But it was hard work, in castes where "reading comes" not even to the men, where field and household tasks press hourly. Radha made the discovery that most reformers and educators make sooner or later, that hope lies in the young. Indefatigably she pursued this ray of fresh light.

I stood in her courtyard one morning; a little herd-boy came in; his goats were jostling one another outside in the lane.

"He has come for his lesson," she explained to me; "I shall be ready in a moment to go with you."

From a shelf she reached down a bit of broken slate, wrote two letters, forming one Telugu word, on it and made the boy repeat the sounds after her.

"That is your lesson for to-day; mind you know it to-night," she admonished the small student, who thrust the slate into a bag slung on his back, where it kept company with his midday meal, a few *chapatties* made of *ragi* and a savoury morsel of curried *brinjal.*

"He is my neighbour Venkamma's son; he has to herd all day and there is plenty of time for him to learn while he is out."

"But would everybody see and seize chances with neighbours' sons?" I thought to myself as I watched her sending him off with an encouraging smile, and heard him clicking to his goats to fare forth into the wilderness, and pictured him under a thorn-bush at noon conning over his slate.

Among the women her words sank into a heart here and there. A middle-aged widow of the potter caste, named Naramma, became so deeply impressed that she resolved to brave the wrath and opposition of her world and follow Christ openly. She knew, however, that should she avow her intention beforehand she would probably be prevented by force from carrying it out, so she kept it secret. The day and hour were arranged. By back lanes she arrived at the little church; then the door was closed and the service of baptism took place without interruption. Directly afterwards she went home and told her family. There was an angry scene. Her brother with whom she lived immediately ordered her out of the house and forbade her ever to return. Her old mother fell on the ground weeping. Naramma went out into the yard and sat there alone and hungry while the others had their meal. She did not know where she should now turn; yet a great inward peace sustained her. After dark the old mother crept out to her, clutching a handful of rice which she laid before the daughter whom she would no longer touch.

"I do not want you to starve," she whispered. Naramma accepted it gratefully.

The hour came for Radha's daily evening meeting. I hastened to her house; the room was full, Naramma sat amongst them, her face irradiated by an inner light. We had started singing when the tap, tap of a stick could be heard; someone walking by its aid came nearer. I looked across the room and saw an old woman standing in the doorway, leaning heavily on her stick; her grey hair dishevelled, tears raining down her face. "My mother," whispered Naramma.

"Come in, amma, and sit down with us," Radha invited her.

The words brushed past her, unheeded. She walked across the room and stood in front of me.

"Oh, why, why have you done this thing?" she wept. "Why did you make my daughter break her caste? Why couldn't she have worshipped your God without touching the water? Now shame is upon our family."

"Mother, I must serve God and Jesus Christ who showed the way," broke in Naramma; "it is not shame, it is salvation."

But the old woman could not take in anything new; she only understood that her old loyalties had been outraged, and wept hopelessly.

"Where will my daughter stay now?"

Radha was more than ready to take her in, but to let her live with a Christian advertised the family disgrace publicly; the suggestion was no consolation to the mother. To Radha also the potters closed their doors. Eventually, a relation in another village, astonished at such independence and devotion and wishing to hear more of this way, opened his house to her. And there Naramma, having caught a spark of Radha's fire, influenced him till he, too, was baptized, though it took years to reach that point.

The potters' door did not always remain closed. The day came when Radha took me again to their house. I sat among them while three of the men were beating their pots into shape; the noise was distracting, yet how much it meant to be there and talk to them freely. And Naramma was allowed to pay visits. Sometimes Hinduism seems curiously yielding to anyone presenting a really bold front to it. The old mother, so broken-hearted on the day of baptism, came and sat down by us and listened willingly.

"Do you remember how you wept that day?" I asked.

Her only answer was a happy smile. Five of the potter people came regularly to Radha's meeting. But it needed an unflagging enthusiasm like hers to bring about this change.

* * * * *

The whole town of Bukkuru was mad on the *Mahorram.* It was the last day of this great Mohammedan festival; the noisy, festive crowds were on their way to the *tank*, carrying spears (commemorating the famous fight and death of two successors of the Prophet) to the water; Hindus, always ready for a new feast, joined in the riotous, brilliant procession.

It happened to be one of my visits to Bukkuru.

The town itself was deserted; as no work seemed feasible in the houses and all schools, of course, were closed, I thought of joining the gay occasion and watching the doings of the crowd near the water. I ran down to Radha's house to ask her to come also.

From afar came the sound of pipes and tomtoms, the cries and shouting of the people, but the streets were silent and empty; here and there an old woman sat nodding in the shade of a wall; some pariah dogs, reconnoitring round forsaken kitchens, slunk away at my approach. When nearing Radha's house I could hear subdued voices inside. The door stood ajar, so I gently pushed it open. Three forms were kneeling, their faces bent reverently towards the ground; one woman's voice was speaking slowly, timidly, then Radha's streamed forth in wistful, pleading prayer. I stood on the threshold and listened, strangely stirred. Brilliant sunshine flooded the courtyard; not far off wild excitement, ostensibly in the name of religion, was going on; the noise of shouts and drums cut through the still midday air; now and then a dull thunder, as of a multitude roaring in unison, vibrated across—and here was the quiet, half-dark room and just the two or three Christ had spoken of.

"Have you a meeting at midday, too?" I asked.

"Chalamma often comes in for a few minutes' prayer when she has time," said Radha in a voice so casual that it betrayed the frequency of the occurrence.

My eyes travelled round the little courtyard. A low stool, a first reader, a slate were lying about.

"Who has been reading here?"

"Narainappa. He was having a lesson when Chalamma came in."

Narainappa is the relation who took Naramma in. When visiting Bukkuru he comes to Radha's meetings. The signs of reading lessons reminded me of another one I had come upon.

"How is that little herd-boy Verana whom you taught to read?"

"He has learnt all I could teach him and goes to school now."

"But his mother is a poor coolie woman," I said wonderingly; "can she pay school-fees?"

"No, I pay them," explained Radha.

I said nothing, at least outwardly. But knowing the slenderness of her resources, a mark of admiration was registered mentally.

Chalamma became a dear friend of hers. She had not the courage of Naramma and felt unable to break through the barriers of caste. During her last illness, however, a different scale of values seemed to dawn on her, she begged for baptism and her wish was granted.

Two of her sons were stalwart Hindus; but to the eldest of her children, a man of thoughtful mind, Radha's words came with a deep appeal. She taught him to read, very much in the fashion she had adopted with the little goat-herd, for he had gardens to cultivate, and the noontide heat would often bring a spell of leisure, devoted by most of his companions to sleep. But he learned a higher devotion and caught some of Radha's enthusiasm.

We sat round the camp lantern one evening, Chalamma and her son, Radha and her sister, another convert from the school-teacher caste, talking till late over the "words of this life." At length, as all of us had early morning work, the prolonged talk, drawn forth by the deep interest of the hearers, was brought to a close and we bade one another good night.

"But no rest yet for me," smiled Chalamma's son. "This is the time when some young shepherds I know keep watch over their flocks by night. They like me to come and tell them these things when all is quiet." He went on to speak of his first timid attempts to witness for his Lord in villages of the neighbourhood; his lack of education caused diffidence at first. "I did not think I could tell them," he related. "I was afraid, but the Lord gave me a mouth to speak for Him!"

Little wonder that he has since become a devoted evangelist.

In many Missions it has been found a helpful plan to ask workers to keep diaries, accurate records of work done, of villages or houses visited; and the value of method and regularity is not to be esteemed lightly by any of us. Radha could not keep such records; for though she had learned to read and to sign her name she was innocent of the art of writing beyond that. Innocent, also, of any sense that her work was ever done, that what could be required of her was over for the day.

It was the evening before a 4.45 a.m. departure the next day. I was furiously writing letters in the little Bukkuru rest-house, as we were going to a postless wilderness, when I suddenly bethought myself that a stolen lock had not been replaced. Hastily I ran down to Radha's house to ask her to get me one. She, too, would be busy preparing for the journey, I thought; but to my surprise, heard animated voices in the courtyard.

"Oh, brother, listen to me!" I distinguished her earnest tones as I came nearer. "Listen to these words; they are your life!"

I went in; a cousin from a distant village had arrived with his two wives. A bother and interruption to us ordinary mortals—a heaven-sent opportunity to Radha. How fortunate that she had not gone on this journey already! There was still all the evening in which to appeal to them.

"Have you got your cold rice ready for the journey?" I asked with a smile.

"No, nothing, not even this evening's meal yet—it does not matter. I can do it by midnight. My relatives came in the afternoon, they are listening to these words, they are listening well."

It was ever her foremost thought. Personal needs, personal comforts, never counted in comparison.

This man and his wives were ultimately baptized, one of the wives voluntarily renouncing him; to solve a difficult problem. The two elder daughters are now Christian teachers —the third is Jewel—mentioned elsewhere.[1] Perhaps Radha's mantle of fervour and enthusiasm will descend upon her, and she will have, in addition, the gifts that Christian education can give.

The lack of these was at times perceptible in Radha. Spontaneity and selflessness where she recognized its need were her strong points; but to tact and self-restraint she was less habituated; conscious of her goodwill to everyone she rather expected her earnest and good intention to be understood as such. Human beings, alas, are not always so discerning.

As I arrived in Bukkuru one day and entered the little rest-house she awaited me weeping.

"I am bad, oh I am bad," she sobbed, "and disgraced in the town."

Inquiry elicited that a woman of bad character had come to live in her lane; at first she seemed influenced by Radha's teaching, but then hardened her heart and since then lost no opportunity of heaping abuse on her former instructress. "And I got angry too," confessed Radha. "I reproved her ways, but I thought I could show her how bad they were; yet she would not stop, but called me horrible names—I could not bear it; I ran round to the Registrar to get him to

[1] See pp. 185 and 207 ff. in *An Uphill Road in India.*

keep her quiet—and he . . . and he . . ." here the poor woman choked miserably, "he fined us both eight annas for brawling, —me too!"

I confess to little admiration of the Registrar's power of discernment; one was a woman of notoriously bad character, the other respected throughout the town; but also one was a Hindu, the other held a faith on which Brahmin officials did not look with favour. Had it influenced the verdict? However that might be, in our talk over the matter we thought in the end that perhaps a little training in self-control and greater humility had been the very thing needed and resolved to peg away at that difficult lesson.

Yet again, she could see straight to the heart of a situation, perceiving the chief need. Many were the occasions when her sympathetic insight helped me. One such memory stands out specially clearly.

Without any warning I had been plunged into deep sorrow by the news of the sudden and wholly unexpected home-call of a beloved mother. To spare the daughter abroad the other home folk had refrained from a cable, judging it kinder to send the news only with all possible details. And so letters from the dear one had continued to arrive, welcomed as ordinary blessings, with no hint that they were the last.

Then suddenly the world turned dark and incredible.

Days passed; difficult days of habituating oneself to the sense of a shield and shelter now withdrawn.

Daily life had to go on; the hours brought their claim, duties had to be performed. And so, not many days after, I found myself in Bukkuru.

"I heard of your loss; I am very, very sorry," Radha said simply, yet with such sympathy that my defences of reserve gave way.

"I want to go home! I must see my brothers and sisters!"

She stroked my cheek in silence.

"It is so hard, at a time like this," I began again, "to be so far away. I don't think I can bear it! I need my own people. I must go!"

Her motherly face had been gazing into the distance. Now she turned towards me. Slowly a tender smile irradiated her features, as if an inner light had been lit. I looked at her astonished.

"Feed My sheep," she said; very lovingly, yet with a strange ring of authority. With a gesture that swept the horizon she repeated, "Feed My sheep."

* * * * *

She had a gift I have not met too often in India, that of humour. At the same time she was sometimes like a child in naïve need of appreciation.

A Deputation from England arrived in Andapur and met our Christians. When in friendly converse, after more formal occasions, Radha pulled my sleeve.

"Have you told them about my work?"

"What is she asking you so eagerly?" asked the observing Head of a Society.

"She wants to know if I have told you about her work," I translated. A twinkle lit up the face of the comprehending Foreign Secretary.

"Why, you have talked about nothing else!"

Again I gravely translated. A responsive sparkle shone out in Radha's face and she went off in peals of laughter. "Nothing else?"

* * * * *

After years of much prayer on her behalf the sister in the distant mountain village had come to join Radha's way of life. She showed forth an entirely different side of the Christian character from her sister. Radha was all fire and fervour, action and aggressiveness; in her resolute way she might not always be sufficiently aware of other people's feelings. The younger woman embodied her name, Prema, Love; the sweetest of tempers was hers, the most unselfish of dispositions. Never once through our years of fellowship have I seen her in any other mood but that of sunny serenity, never heard her say one unkind or complaining word against anyone. Everybody loved Prema. On our tours together many a villager would say to Radha, "Teach us more, come again and teach us"; to Prema they said, "Please stay here and live with us." The elder sister had the greater gifts and the stronger character, the deeper zeal and love for others, also the as yet more undisciplined self-will. But her humility was ever ready too.

We three were on our way to a village one morning; for some reason Radha had fallen behind; Prema and I arrived without her and entered the house of a shepherd woman, who spread a mat for us on her little verandah. We started talking; presently Radha strode in, the seat convenient for talking to the women was occupied by Prema; instinctively, in her eagerness to speak to them, Radha moved towards it, and equally instinctively, and wholly unobtrusively, Prema vacated it.

"Might not Prema have the good seat for once?" I whispered jokingly to Radha. Instantly she recognized her lack of thought: "Oh, my sister," she said in the frankest and sweetest way, "thou art better than I." The missionary sitting by thought she might well learn from both!

In India elder sisters occupy a position of authority. Younger sisters do not address them by their names, but as "*Akka*," elder sister. An *akka* calls the children of her younger sister "son" and "daughter," not nephew and niece, and as a matter of course orders them about. Perhaps it might have been better for Radha's all-round spiritual development had she been born the younger. (Thus do we all like to put our suggestive spokes into the government of the universe!)

With most of us motives are apt to be a little mixed. Zeal and fervour, a little bossiness, even—who knows?—a little desire to show off,

"some self-congratulation, soft and sly,"

might at times have got entangled in Radha's inner roots; while fearing to judge, one fears also to give unbalanced praise; though, personally, I give unstinted admiration.

It was the morning after a night disturbed by red ants; these little pests had overrun the tent in their millions, stinging us all into restless wakefulness and consequent fatigue the next day. Work had to be done all the same; we were due in a village four miles away where we toiled till midday. On the return journey some wayfarers caught up with us as the bulls, drawing our uncovered cart, ploughed slowly through the sand.

"Look, Prema, there are people coming behind you," Radha pointed out to her sister, who was sitting at the end, facing in the direction we were going. "Should you not tell them something?"

Now doing things on your own initiative, and doing them to order, are two very different things; Prema, indeed, obediently faced round, but her attempt to establish conversational openings with the strangers was somewhat halting and timid—too slow for her *akka's* fervent spirit—or was there, possibly, a hidden consciousness, "I can do it better"?

"I must get down and talk to them," she said eagerly, and stopped the cart. In the delay of her scrambling out the travellers got well ahead, but she ran till she caught them up and trudged with them through the hot noon, hunger and fatigue and heat forgotten in her zeal to expound to them the message entrusted to her. "I might never see those people again," she said afterwards.

Back in camp and after a meal I thought we all deserved a rest; but a teacher came, burdened with many affairs; during the prolonged interview with him I heard voices not far off, and presently Radha marched in with a beaming face: "I have just had such a feast."

"Yes?" I said, knowing her ways. "Then to whom have you been talking now?"

"Shepherd people over there; they were taking their midday rest under that tree."

"And do you not want a midday rest?"

"I was filled with desire to talk to them."

That same day when returning at sundown to the tent after an afternoon's work in the village where the interest of the hearers had led to talking till the point of exhaustion, we passed through some fields. At some distance coolie women were still busy on the threshing-floors; they called to us across the intervening spaces of unreaped grain: "Where have you come from? What is your work?"

One member of the party was for a brief reply and for passing on; but not so Radha. The glow in her heart was fanned into flame at once by the casual inquiry.

"Are you not winnowing?" she called back, as she carefully made her way towards them on the narrow mud dams between the fields; developing in her talk their occupation into a parable as she went; those women were not left in doubt about her work and her message; and that other member of the party stood by and gave thanks to God for such a spirit, surely pure gold of devotion and enthusiasm, in spite of little human alloys now and then.

Or it might gleam forth in personal habits. Like most Indians, she was an inveterate chewer of betel-nut; the little pestle and mortar for pounding it hung ever at her girdle, and many a conversation was interrupted by the need for pounding, chewing, and the inevitable conclusion: ejecting the chewed remainder, which is never swallowed.

A missionary visited her once and, when leaving, still stood in conversation, her hand on Radha's arm, so that she, in politeness, did not have the desired opportunity of getting rid of the betel in her mouth. Without warning the visitor added, "Let us pray before I go," and immediately knelt down, Radha following her example, but obliged to remain dumb herself. After the missionary's departure she stood still and reflected.

"This wretched betel-nut caused me embarrassment and perhaps disappointment to the missionary. I could not speak to God with her because of it. I could not even properly follow her prayer, I was uncomfortable because of the betel in my mouth. Then—never shall there be betel in my mouth again! It has hindered prayer once; it will not hinder it twice." She did not even wait to sell her pestle and mortar, but threw it away that very day into a deep water-channel. Inveterate smokers or tea drinkers may perhaps gauge her sacrifice, though not wholly; for betel-chewing accustoms the digestion to it and it becomes a necessity. Yet from that day she never touched it again. "God has taken away my taste for it," she said triumphantly later; "at first it was difficult, but I do not want it now."

The sick in her neighbourhood knew her well; she was not great in preaching only. Every need appealed to her. "I shall be a little late," she explained one day. "I promised to bathe the new baby in the potters' house; the relative who was to come and help has not arrived."

At what sacrifice in money and trouble she saved a motherless baby from being sold by her own father to prostitutes has been told elsewhere [1]; also how the beloved younger sister died during an epidemic of cholera.[2] It was a deep and lasting grief to Radha.

She is old now; the discovery that her body no longer obeys her eager behests was a hard discipline to her; that

[1] *An Uphill Road in India*, pp. 205–207. [2] *Ibid.*, p. 163.

active and enthusiastic spirit could with difficulty learn the lesson of accepting, instead of rendering, service. Eyesight failed her, and she had ever been a tireless reader of one great Book! An operation partly restored it.

At the time of writing she is awaiting her home-call, in her impetuous way sometimes upbraiding the Lord for being so slow. Perhaps the Lord knows what He is about, perhaps He is perfecting that which concerns her and adding to her faith patience; but when the call comes, one may be sure that she will meet it with her old alacrity, and that a very abundant entrance will be prepared for one who sought so long and so tirelessly, and when she found would not be saved alone.

"Therefore to her it was given,
Many to save with herself."

CHAPTER XVI

SECRET BREAD

THE bigger girls had Hebrews xi. for their lesson to-day. "By faith Noah . . ," "By faith Moses . . ."; these splendid stories of solitary courage are perhaps too well known to them. The sunny afternoon went by while they listened open-mouthed to modern continuations: "By faith Pandita Rama Bai . . ," "By faith Father Damien . . ," "By faith David Livingstone . . ," "By faith his black servants . . ."

We all like stories. And then we have our longings. But to translate them into life is a different matter. So at least I find it.

"How is it that you have no faith?" asked Christ of men scared by the sight of towering waves.

I wonder what He expected them to have. The confident expectation that laws of nature were plastic and malleable? That circumstances are conquerable?

Certainly the disciples knew that the use of known laws could alter material things, as fire affects metal, or clay, or water. Were they expected to believe in still higher laws, sharing their Master's amazing confidence in the nearness of the spiritual order? Their nation's history might have taught them something. But perhaps better than history these men knew winds and waves and their power to destroy. They knew little of the incalculable forces of another kingdom—what, indeed, do we? We still simply, if arrogantly, deny "miracles of power." Will it still take centuries before "miracles" become natural occurrences to Christian people?

The material and visible are certainly to the fore. That circumstances are not our masters, but our subjects I find a hard lesson to learn.

> "Things are in the saddle
> And ride mankind"

complained Emerson. And many of us with him.

I was due to leave for our Church and Mission conferences, and had been told to bring a servant. But the man had got himself entangled in a court case; it was to come on some days ago, but then postponed till the very day of my departure. I sent to ask the Magistrate kindly to give the case precedence, as the servant must leave with me at 4 p.m. "All right," was the reply. But when the servant went to court in the morning the Magistrate had gone off to Penuroy, and the case was postponed for a further two days. This is quite usual and convenient to the magistrate or to clients who ask for delay, but not to other people. I had to leave Rama Das behind and take a raw and untrained new-comer, and say to the little lapping waves of worry, "begone! we shall manage."

In the train, by appointment, a former teacher joined me further down the line. She is married to a wastrel whose trading always comes to nothing; now she is working in a Government school. She was a splendid little evangelist in former days; in her present appointment there is no way of direct spiritual service. Is this all life is to hold? They have no children. Why not try wholeheartedly Mission work and take the headmistress-ship of our Dharmpalli school? Her eyes shone with longing as I propounded the needs there.

"I want to come. I must think. I will let you know. He will be against it."

"But you are earning for you both? Does not, then, the power of choice of a post rest with you?"

"Yes, I earn our living. And so, you see . . . less money. . . ."

"But freedom to work for God?"

"Ye–es. Still, one must live. I will ask."

If the path of faith looked steep to her (too steep, it proved in the end) it does to others as well.

"Look at our desperate state. In the men's work; in the women's work," was the topic that depressed us even more than the heat and dust, as a number of us travelled through the blazing noon next day over a stony *ghaut* road and a mile wide river-bed of blistering sand at its end. On arrival at the Mission station it was still the same; news of quarrels and scandals was waiting. "And only such a small missionary staff now," lamented my hostess. "And only God left to help us," I could not forbear adding. The response was immediate: "Rather a big Remainder!"

But in our Church Council next day the same battle-line stood arrayed against that inner attitude. Our Indian helpers are now in charge alongside of missionaries; indeed, in democratically constituted councils like ours, they may be said to form the government, as brown outnumbers white. Are we expecting too much? There appears to be a certain obtuseness to spiritual values or claims. The pastorate of a weak church was vacant, and no volunteer could be found in that assembly. "There are factions there; they will talk against the pastor." My thoughts strayed to South Sea islanders; how many of those heroic native teachers had volunteered to go to other islands and endured there loneliness and danger, some of them being martyred in the end, and belonging to that succession of whom the world is not worthy. To be sure, they had seen it happen to some missionaries first. Oh for some cannibals in India! I felt tempted to sigh. If a few of us were slain that would help greatly. But when discouragement threatened to gain the victory the signs of the Divine Spirit striving within the spirit of man became manifest. A worker stood up and declared his readiness to go to that difficult church and face the contradiction of sinners said to be so rife there.

Our own business meetings followed and were depressing enough; anxious re-arrangements, to meet the curtailments in staff and finance. They lasted all day, from 8 a.m. till 6 p.m. Then from six o'clock till eight I was hard at work on a minute that had to be presented next morning. It was; but after reading it and embodying the emendations suggested, I had to leave the meeting as temperature had crept up to 104. Merely over-fatigue, but "how shall I travel to-morrow?" a wave lapped near again. However, I had not to bother to beat it back; a small whisper said clearly, "It will be all right"; and so it proved. Though still 102 in the evening, I woke refreshed after a good night, gaily rose and packed, then fell on the minute again, partly dictated, partly copied, it; able for everything, including the whole tiring journey back.

In the evening I arrived at the junction, where the catechist met me to arrange about a women's Summer School. Sudden rain! I had brought no coat; but, undaunted, draped myself in a red table-cloth and proceeded in the dark to the little room behind the church, where I spent the night, the coolie having learned the ways of camp-cots, bedding, and supper fairly creditably by this time. The planned interview took place and details were worked out satisfactorily; but next morning, just at train time, it poured afresh. In the daytime a figure arrayed in a red table-cloth would look a little remarkable, I feared, but stalked brazenly through the downpour nevertheless and survived, along with the spectators, who may have found it more difficult.

At Andapur the girls' class was waiting, also an accumulated post; also visitors had arrived, old Krishnagi's widow and her daughter and sister whom she wants taken into the Home; Rama Das, his court case over, was yearning to pour out his indignation over a fine—while I, still a little wobbly after the fever, had rather hoped for a day's quiet to prepare for the impending Summer School.

"I object to everlasting climbing, I want to sit down," I used to say. Somehow, these days I don't feel like saying it. There is a sense of being carried. I cannot explain it. In the midst of everything, "the secret."

* * * * *

It is needed.

> "Though with thine earliest dawn thou shouldest begin it
> Scarce were it ended with thy setting sun."

Here we are at Ramidi bungalow, for the Summer School. And here is trouble.

Never before had I found the bungalow occupied, so had blithely counted on the Bible-woman and girls having one room, myself the other, the village women all the outhouses. But when we arrived there was a crowd in possession. A Survey Officer had the whole bungalow stuffed with his travelling outfit; fifteen lascars camped in the outhouses; the space between these and the back verandah was strewn with their things; there seemed no room for anyone anywhere. It was getting dark; we were all tired and thirsty after the midday start and the two-mile walk from the station, during which I had managed to get both heels blistered. Instead of rest and spreading ourselves comfortably—confusion. In a hole again! I thought. But experience has taught me that holes are negative things. Certainly they gape at one like idiots; but treated as unreal, they sink away; lo, slopes appear on either hand, they become thoroughfares! Three little rooms, dirty and full of rubbish, were discovered at the back of the outhouses; these were swept out and cleaned for the village women; one room in the bungalow was made available for the rest of us, and some could sleep in the verandah. Gradually a chair and a table and a basin were obtained. Moreover, when the young Survey Officer returned he welcomed me like a long-lost mother; it turned out that our arrival was the way out of *his* hole! One servant, used only to towns, had deserted him a few days ago; the sole remaining prop was lying down with fever, and his master had not known what to do for a meal. A little after nine o'clock we sat down to one together.

Next morning the remainder of the village women

arrived. They are Christians from villages near, all belonging to the outcaste section of the community, and woefully ignorant and backward. After the morning class with them discouragement assailed me. I had not expected much, but *such* dullness and slowness were beyond expectations. No spark of interest or response lit up their eyes; the meeting fell absolutely flat. And yet I had been so sure that the inception of this Summer School (which I had seen successfully carried out elsewhere) was not mine, but of One who did not mean it to be a failure. We must find a new method of approach, I thought; maybe, the Bible-woman will find it better? So I left her to it; but she also complained of inattention, though they liked the girls' singing.

And then, at the next meeting, their complete attention was gained. Light was in their eyes, attention did not waver for a moment. Merely by teaching them through their eyes instead of only through their ears.

"A blind man came to Jesus." . . . "Jivamma (to a Boarding Home girl), go out, come back with your eyes shut, calling out, 'Lord, I want sight!'" Jivamma did. Right through the selected stories we acted them. The girls, trained by their weekly drama, caught the spirit at once; the women, having seen the story happen before them, exerted themselves to learn the lyric describing it. When our Ramidi schoolgirls came up in the afternoon, providing both further actors and audience, the interest increased. The village women liked seeing others instructed, and in case they wearied there were interruptions. A loudly wailing low-caste villager arrived; he had been beaten by a caste man and demanded to have his wrong righted. He was dispatched with a note to the Police Inspector; not in order to make a case, but to gain future protection by a warning to the caste people. Also a girl from our school pulled at my sleeve to get a hearing for her concerns; a *Bogum* child, anxious to go on with her education and live a decent life. One of how many!

So instruction went on as life does, with little semblance to method and order, yet—let us hope—educating us all the time. When everyone had departed in the evening for cooking preparations I stretched myself in a camp-chair in the verandah; and then my neighbour, returned from surveying, emerged from the next room and sat down for a chat. Here was trouble again. No direct confidences were made, but from hints dropped I gathered that a woman had broken faith, and now he was losing faith in everything. He proved to be extraordinarily thoughtful, delving for a solution to his problems. To add to his causes for dejection he had received warning that the Government axe of economy might affect him; he belonged to the military, which apparently he hated, and joined the survey, which he liked, "so good to *do* things"—but now he may be "curtailed"! His Damocles' sword descended the very next day when his post arrived; so in the evening, after another long day with the women, he and I went for a walk in the gloaming and discussed the universe.

"But who, who, thinks things like that?" he said perplexedly.

"I do," I asserted stoutly; "and there is an army of others who do—else how did I learn?"

"I never met them," he lamented. Conventional Christianity had stumbled him badly. As his servant is still ill we continue to meet at meal-times. His men were admirably respectful to the women and girls; and the whole Summer School went without a hitch.

If I had been told beforehand that an officer with fifteen lascars would occupy the bungalow at the very time fixed for it I should have given up the plan for lost. Yet it was carried out without a sense of strain, new friends were made, and I am personally the richer for all its memories. "In quietness and confidence . . ." Though *my* post the same day brought the disturbing news that a hitch had occurred in the renting of a bungalow considered securely taken for the next holiday.

Horrid wave, that; for hill holidays are beloved. But are they beyond the attention of that higher Kingdom? "Give us this day our daily bread," and if a holiday is part of that it will not fail.

Nor did it. In answer to my remonstrance a reply came saying it was a mistake and they meant to keep the agreement.

* * * * *

And here I am, in the blessed cool, and other marvels.

> "I know a bank where the wild thyme grows,
> Where the oxslip and the nodding violet blows. . . ."

But I know a ledge where the eagle goes, O Oberon, though Titania would certainly not "sleep there some time of a night"; it is advisable to keep awake in my eyrie. One reaches it by walking along the edge of a high grass-land, falling off sheerly into precipices; where a ravine interrupts the stretch of table-land I step carefully down over the side, warily descending from tussock to tussock, till a few yards down the shade of a perpendicular rock is reached; there a ledge makes a seat. Friendly grass still grows on the slope in front of me for a little way farther down, giving the sense of a nice safe hill-side and preventing tremors. But it ends abruptly in an edge and a sheer drop of 2,000 feet. (I have looked at it from the other side of that great amphitheatre.) There you sit, world hid and world lost, in an awesome semicircle of sheer space; depth of air below you, heights of it above you: a vast emptiness across to the ramparts opposite—"spatial thunder!" I whispered in awe. The evening shadows were in the valleys; the high table-land lay in the sun's rays still. The blue carpet of thick jungle far below, where I could hear monkeys crying and jungle sheep barking hoarsely, looked misty and awful in that terrible depth; the crags unmovedly reared heavenwards, the water roared over the rocks in the ravine close by. In the *shola* by my side swifts darted about; cloudlets, just born, kissed the rocks opposite. An eagle was sailing, sailing, over abysmal spaces, never stirring a feather. There one sat on the edge of Infinity, and thought lost itself.

On what other borders of Infinity are our lives lived? That eagle, achieving the—to us—impossible, is he a creature of nobler capacities than we? Or, in that other realm of potencies we so readily deny, could we also—even now—achieve undreamt-of conquests over matter? That capacity of the soul called faith, is that meant to establish a connection which would bring unseen legions to our aid, would, for instance, help missionaries to triumph over financial limitations? or, at all events, to be always serene in face of them, knowing that the progress of the Kingdom of God, which is always within, cannot be hindered by lack of outward means?

The next afternoon I walked out to the rampart beyond my eyrie; there I lay in the long soft grass, the afternoon sun shining on me so warmly that my face tingled. Then, without warning, mists stole up, in a few moments the wide amphitheatre before me, purple and deep, had disappeared; instead, there moved a sea, unbounded, intangible, of grey and white, while I still lay in warm sunshine above it. In front, beside, below—Mystery. The sun was sinking towards a range of firs standing against the sky; the mists rose higher; a marvel happened, the sun turned into a moon. Wintrily the firs loomed through a haze, the veil spread over all the fir woods, the whole landscape became wintry, a cold and silvery moon (i.e. sun) glittered palely behind the firs, with unblinded eyes I looked straight into the lifeless silver ball; the light behind the firs was as the light of moonrise. And right overhead all the time stood the real moon—two silver balls in the sky at the same time! Then one of them dipped and disappeared; at that moment the sea of mist in front reft, the tangible earth loomed visible again, and dark cool depths of jungle showed below. I got up to go home, turned again for a look, a few shreds of mists clung to distant ranges, and then the whole scene turned itself into fairyland before my eyes, flooded by unhindered moonlight. A breeze sprang up, carrying the sound of a far-off bell—the Angelus in the Roman Catholic church. The tall grasses on the high table-land stirred and rippled; I, too, bowed in worship.

> "From above us and from under,
> In the ocean and the thunder
> Thou preludest to the wonder
> Of Thy paradise to be;
> For a moment we may guess Thee
> From Thy creatures that confess Thee
> When the morn and even bless Thee,
> And Thy smile is on the sea." [1]

[1] F. W. H. Myers, *Sunrise*.

CHAPTER XVII

GOLDEN LEAVES

THE morning, and the evening—what simple words; what infinite contents! Yet each day holds both.

One morning, on a holiday in the Palni mountains, I stood soon after dawn on the hills I have christened "The Neighbours," being next to our bungalow which is out in the wilds, two miles from the Hill Settlement itself. From "The Neighbours" (there are two, the Old Man, slightly higher than the Old Woman), one looked down into Shembaganur and other valleys, towards the peak of Perumal and many chains of hills, one behind the other, on one side; on the other towards the Pillar Rocks and the ranges towards Travancore. But on that day the green and purple valleys and mountains had vanished; in their stead arctic fields of driven snow spread before me, their pure white broken up into crevasses and glaciers and frozen waves; towards the horizon wild fantastic shapes and boulders were piled up into solid icebergs. These Polar regions swept right from Perumal, looming faintly through illuminated sunny white masses, round the hill on which I stood, into the valleys on my right, and away and away in front over the whole expanse of plains. A crag, rooted solidly in the plain, now and then stoutly stuck its summit through the whiteness, but only succeeded in appearing faint and ghostlike; solidity, firmness, reality, belonged to the wild and snowy world of Alps. The "Neighbours" lay in radiant sunshine; behind me the downs were gleaming and laughing, while below stretched this extraordinary cloud effect. After an hour the fields of ice and snow began to lose their hold on solidity and to look what they were; the astonishing fairyland slowly vaporized. But what a morning of splendid wastefulness! A miracle of beauty, and no Artist watching to see if anyone took note of it. Or was there Some One?

His exhibitions go on. Back in the house, I settled myself with twenty-four foolscap pages of Telugu writing, examination papers to be appraised and marked. All of a sudden the radiant sunshine disappeared, as if Autumn had entered. Clouds enveloped the house, white mists drove past the windows; the tall blue gums loomed through like tired ghosts. At times the vapours thickened and shut out the trees altogether, then thinned a little above, and an even more mysterious sight presented itself. Spectral and foundationless branches swayed above like a world of lost and restless spirits, into which I gazed with awe and curiosity; while drip, drip, the rain beat on the zinc roof. Again all grew opaque and a high wall of white surrounded the house; mists were standing solid and still by the window; they moved, and I could see the rosebush again, then the willow-gum in the valley, the cattle browsing in the grass, then—all vanished. Drip, drip, on the roof; thunder among the hills, and—whatever is this? Islands swimming up? Mountains emerging from the sea? All the world is sea—all the world from my window, anyway, the Flood must be on. Here is Ararat poking up—no, the sea has swallowed it again. Who can do papers? Ararat endureth! The white hosts are fleeing; radiant plains gleam again in the North, and green and dark and silver is the South. Oh, who will o'er the downs with me? Balefully the unread sheets glower at me.

But in the afternoon I sallied forth into a rainy world, climbed a hill half-way and followed a "fireline" round it, through woods. A heavy crackle of boughs on my right froze me into immovability. No bird would make so much noise—could it be samber? Jungle sheep? Two black shapes appeared. Wild pigs! Father and Mother careered across the line just in front of me, their nursery after them; one, two, three—but the last pigling lost its head; perhaps I moved and frightened it, it galloped along the path, instead of crossing after the others. Away I streaked after it. A silly longing to catch a little wild pig inspired the chase; but however madly I tore through the wet jungle Young Pig won the Derby and disappeared; perhaps it was as well, the tusks of an angry Father Boar might not be an advisable acquaintance. I struck across the downs, got into bogland in which green tussocks as high as my hip sat lazily about; with the aid of my stick I crossed from green boulder to boulder and gained firm hillside. All around me was the quiet grey world of the downs, sombre and silent; but here and there lay golden patches where holes in the clouds let bits of sun through. I found a rock, shining wet, of course; a folded scarf made it habitable. What an evening! Behind me the woods were singing loudly; the great Pillar Rocks stood straight and threatening; the little grassy valleys gave forth the sound of madly twittering birds and the scent of madly fragrant grass and thyme. My hillside faced West; little clumps of acacia- and gum-trees stood on the opposite hill between me and the Western sky. The sun was going down behind a solid wall of cloud now, taking no notice of anything or anybody. But between the lower horizontal edge of the cloud-wall and the skyline of the hill below it there was a gap, about an inch. Wherefore, suddenly,

> "Red out glared the sun, like knight from leaguered town."

In a second, a myriad slender leaves in the acacia- and gum-trees sprang to attention; shot at horizontally, hit with gold, trembling, shaking, rustling, preening—the incredibly radiant little army saluted their queen. Two minutes, three, —then the sun dipped below the hill and the leaves went soberly to bed. But they had had their moment, and so had I.

> "When the golden leaves did flicker,
> And the loving thoughts came thicker
> And the thrill of life beat quicker. . . ."

The sharp tang of evening came into the clear rain-washed

air. A jungle sheep, stepping daintily and noiselessly, strayed quite close up before it perceived me—then what bounding leaps! I turned home through the rapidly oncoming dusk, to the cheerful blaze of a wood-fire and the welcome of friendly voices. Also of letters—but them I eyed askance.

Forebodings were justified. Perhaps I had been too righteously pleased that exam. papers had been dispatched and that there would be peace? Heavy rain in Bukkuru had brought down the roof of the Mohammedan school there bodily; it had fallen on all the furniture, maps, pictures, books, etc. One after the other wrote about it; where were they to keep school? Apparently they would like me to post them a house. Andapur came in no wise second in the race for thrills. Dorcas wrote that thieves had broken into the storeroom of the Boarding Home and stolen three of the four sacks of rice, each containing forty *seers*. Well, let us be thankful they left us one!

But I must confess I like the Government plan of placing someone in charge when an official goes on leave. Luckless missionaries hump their burdens with them when they go on holiday.

But memories remain. In dusty and crowded days there are still moments when golden leaves flicker suddenly.

So it happened one evening.

Through the dust stirred up by the carts passing along the road, and still more by the trampling herds of buffaloes and cattle moving slowly bazarwards, I was walking home after a long afternoon of visits in Indian homes. Reception there had been varied; in some, indignation and malice against their neighbours had been met; in some, engrossing care for daily bread; in some, worry about the future; in most, a measure of interest in the visitor and her words; and in all, friendliness and politeness, manifested according to the pretty Eastern custom in gifts of flowers.

Garlands of jasmine and marigolds dangled from my arm;

as I walked along I bestowed these, in small sections, on children I met; women with baskets of cowdung carefully collected in the wake of the cattle also stopped to ask for portions and went on with a friendly salaam of thanks. For though flowers are beloved of all not everyone can afford the *pice* the flower-seller demands; yet how good to feel the back knob of hair ornamented by even a few fragrant white or golden blossoms twisted in!

Only a handful of these remained now in my fingers, just enough for one more gift. I peered along the road for another recipient. Dusk was falling, the herds and their guardians had all passed, the road seemed empty. But as I hesitated for a moment before taking the lane leading to the Mission compound another wayfarer came in sight. A thin brown boy, a belated goat-herd, naked to the waist, only a rag of dirty cloth twisted round his middle. He stared at me in alarm; dismay gathered on his face as he saw me lift a hand and beckon to him, palm outwards, fingers curling quickly downwards—the unmistakable gesture that says louder than any words: "Come here!" Full of fear he stood still on his side of the road, evidently longing to bolt, but not daring to. What could the white person over there want? Why did she keep on beckoning? Timidly he obeyed and crept nearer, evidently calculating nervously how close he might come and yet keep out of reach; his poor little thin body could be seen almost trembling with apprehension as he unwillingly responded to that wordless beckoning. At last he stood before me, lifting frightened eyes to scan the face of the white stranger. Without a word the flowers were held out to him. It took him a moment to realize the intention; then his hand moved doubtfully upwards. The flowers were dropped into his open palm. "For you," I said.

Then he looked up again. The child's face was transfigured. Rapture shone from his eyes. It was as if the sun had broken through a bank of dark clouds. The change from terror and apprehension could not yet be believed. The light grew and spread in his face; one could almost see the frightened little soul behind it saying, "Is that what you meant? I thought—I feared . . ."

Forgotten are other details of that afternoon and of many afternoons, but the glory of the smile of trust with which we parted has come down the years with me.

Will our unacknowledged terrors, our secret fears, be met one day, thus? Is, even now, a Hand beckoning to us the intention of which we persist in mistaking?

As though God did beseech you. . . ."

* * * * *

Then again, in the silk-weaver's house in Dharmpalli. Round Tulsamma, who lived in it, there was darkness. Neighbours came in for a friendly chat; the hot sun blazed, or the fruit-bringing rains fell; the tall, dung-plastered grain-baskets reaching from floor to ceiling were filled to the top with rice in the husk; the scarlet or orange hanks of raw silk her husband brought her to spin that he might weave them into dazzling *saris* made a gay radiance in the room—she saw naught of it all. Beauty and wealth and human kindliness had lost their savour.

She lived with sorrow. Four dear little children, one after the other, had been taken from the silk-weaver's wife.

The Bible-woman visited her and spoke words of hope; in vain.

"Our eldest girl went to your school, she learned well, my Naraini. She came home very proud one day, your Miss had praised her. She gave her a doll. When your Miss comes to our town bring her to me. Yes, your words are good. I hear them. But they cannot come to me. Nothing can come to me any more."

When I came it was the same. The sad listless face of the bereaved Indian mother remained sad and listless.

"You remember my Naraini?" was ever her question. I did; and do.

"And then Bima?" Yes, the little four-year-old, toddling after her sister, had made her mark in my memory. But no words of mine had power to pierce the darkness of desolation.

"My *Karma* is bad. God is angry with me. He took all, all."

Still, she craved for sympathy.

"She will not let me be without coming to her even for one day," explained the Bible-woman. "She would be hurt if you came to this town without visiting her.

We gave her what we could, unstinted sympathy.

Sometimes, rarely, we ventured to hint that the living had claims, the husband, the mother living with them.

"I wish she could be a little cheerful just sometimes," sighed the grandmother. "The neighbours won't come here any more; they say she only weeps and it is unlucky."

A furlough to England interrupted my visits for a year.

"You will see a great change in the weaver's house," the Bible-woman told me when I came to Dharmpalli again. "The husband has been very ill and had to go away for an operation."

I listened in consternation. "What? That trouble too? Let us go to her at once."

To my amazement an eager, cheerful woman greeted me.

"Come in, come in; it is many days! I want to tell you. He was bad, my man, very bad. The doctor said: 'Take him to the hospital at Andapur.' But that is not a Mission hospital. I was afraid. I said to my husband: 'They of the Mission speak good words, let us go to their hospital, though the journey is longer.' He agreed, though the ticket cost many rupees. He had to have an operation. But I was not afraid. I had seen others go in and have operations. Always they had prayer first. A boy came, he looked dreadful; so wasted and thin, his arms and legs like sticks. Only his stomach swollen like a mountain, you would think he must burst. They cut out a lump, the doctor showed us afterwards. They always show you there what they remove, because people think it is demons they have inside. You would never believe that people can have inside what the doctor takes out without killing them. It is because they pray."

"So you went to their prayers?" I asked.

"There was no need to go; they bring their prayers to you. Every Sunday morning they bring them to each ward. They put a table with a white cloth and flowers; all come, doctors and nurses, and stand and sing and say good words. It is like God coming. I used to be by my husband's bed and listen and then go with them to the other wards and listen again. A girl came, bigger than my Naraini. Her mother cried before the operation. I told her she need not be afraid. They have God there. Her child got better."

As she related her experiences a smile stole out on her face at the wonderful memories. I gazed almost in awe. I had never seen her smile. To watch that sorrowful countenance now glowing with many remembrances seemed like one of the miracles of old.

The grandmother sat by and nodded happily. "She is changed since she went to the hospital. Some comfort came to her in that place. It must be as she says, they have God there."

"*Not far from any one of us,*" I thought, greatly moved. "Not far from the Indian Mother, and her tears—O *God of all Hope!*"

CHAPTER XVIII

A SOLITARY

It was on the evening of a strange little dinner-party that I first met him. An odd circle—the Christian Postmaster, our friend Rangavachari, the Hindu lawyer and reformer, a Eurasian lady, and myself met at Helen Powell's house at Penuroy. To enliven the proceedings the presence of the local musical genius, called *the fiddle achari* by the public, had also been requested; he accompanied impartially the Indian guests who sang lyrics, and the Western women contributing English hymns, the metre and melody of which he picked up notwithstanding their strangeness to his ear. More orthodox Brahmins assembled in the verandah to hear this concert, though they all left when dinner was announced. The meal, though entirely vegetarian, was served, at the Indians' proposal, in Western fashion; instructions in the use of spoons and forks amused hosts and guests alike, and the evening was passing very pleasantly; the various elements of Christian, Hindu, and Theosophic atmospheres blending for the time being harmoniously enough.

But sharp contrasts are never far off in India. When after dinner we went back to the verandah a young Hindu came in, looking much perturbed.

"Such trouble, such trouble," he sighed. "They trouble me, they will not let me do as I think right."

Then, seeing a social party, he controlled his utterance.

"Mr. Nanjandappa, a teacher here," Helen Powell introduced him to me. There was not much chance of private conversation that evening; but we all had become conscious that broadmindedness and friendliness were no longer the predominant note. Next morning he came to see me at the traveller's bungalow where I was staying, and I learned something of his history.

By birth he belonged to a priestly family of the Lingaits, and among his own caste people would have held a high position. In a Mission High school he had learned of Christ; he studied the Christian Scriptures further and became more and more attracted to Him. Hesitatingly he had considered the question of baptism, but got no further. He entered the Government educational service and was sent to a post in Penuroy. There he met Vijaya Ranga, the convert from the Naidu caste, whose flaming zeal and overflowing joy stirred the glowing embers in the young Lingait's heart into lively fire. Correspondence with a missionary ensued and it was settled that his baptism should take place.

But intolerable domestic trouble followed. His young wife should have been sent to him, but her people refused to let her come. His definite intention to be baptized he had kept secret, fearing forcible intervention; but the suspicions that had fallen on him through his friendship with Vijaya Ranga sufficed to place him under a cloud. Until he should clear himself she would not be sent. Well, for her he was willing to wait patiently; but the daily and hourly trouble was his mother. She lived with him and offered fierce and relentless opposition. Few, out of India, can understand how deeply the inner roots of loyalty and devotion, inherent in women everywhere, twine in Hindu hearts round religion and caste, inseparably bound together. If a man would distinguish between them and extricate himself from their tyranny they throw out choking tendrils.

"My mother follows me in the street, and abuses me in public," he said pathetically. "And she is only suspicious now; I do not know what will happen when she knows I am resolved to be a Christian."

He was quite determined to hold on to his purpose, nevertheless.

To my great regret I could not prolong my visit to Penuroy; but the following details were afterwards told me by Helen Powell.

One day in the school he accidentally dropped a letter from the missionary, with whom he had been corresponding. A fellow-teacher picked it up and read in it of his intention to be baptized. He went and told the mother. A furious uproar ensued. Neighbours came in and listened to her wild accusations shrilled out to the air; then she ran wailing through the streets, pouring forth vituperations against her son to any who would hear—and who would not stop and hear in an Indian bazar? Her son might do anything he liked, worship demons, consort with harlots, become an atheist, anything,—as long as he did not break caste.

News came to Helen Powell that he was being kept a prisoner in the house by caste people; but by the time she came to see he had been allowed to go to his work in the school. She followed him there and asked him to come and see her during the midday recess. He promised this, but to her attempts at cheer and encouragement he made no reply; he seemed too bewildered and troubled by the ill-will and opposition round him to be able to take in what she said. However, he came at midday. Unfortunately, she happened to be upstairs for a moment; before she had descended, the mother, following her son, had reached the house and stood at the door shouting foul abuse of the Englishwoman. Unable to bear this Nanjandappa went out and took her home. Crowds of Brahmins then poured into the verandah, and when Helen Powell expressed a wish to follow Nanjandappa they began to argue with her and to dispute his need of being baptized. They even begged her to use her influence to prevent this step. To such a promise (she is not a missionary) she would in no wise consent, on the contrary plainly stated that she would encourage him to stand by his convictions, whatever they were.

"Better have him here and let him say before us all what his convictions are," she suggested.

"Yes, that would be a good thing," they agreed. "We will all come at five o'clock when school is over and bring him here."

On this understanding they at last departed, leaving her thankful for the respite; they had been arguing with her for close on three hours.

The hour fixed approached and she sat waiting. Time passed. No one came. The suspicion crept over her that as she had not proved willing to discourage him from baptism they had no intention of letting him come back to her. A man arrived and looked round as if astonished, then said, "He has not come? I will go and call him," and disappeared. Presently another man came, said the same thing and went off. She waited on, and yet a third man turned up and encouraged her to wait still longer.

Then she learned that Nanjandappa was still at school. "They won't let him leave," added her informer. She immediately set out for the school. On the way she passed Nanjandappa's house. His old mother sat by the courtyard door.

"Where is your son?" asked Helen Powell.

The Hindu mother looked at her with a face of stone.

"I have no son," she muttered, and turned away.

As the Englishwoman entered the school the sight that met her was poor Nanjandappa apparently in a state of mental or physical collapse. A fellow-teacher had put his arm round him, supporting him. They had closed in upon him directly school had been dismissed. He was not a man of great force of will or clear independent thought; when they attacked him with the constant reiteration of the argument that he might serve Christ in private as much as he liked, but without breaking caste, he became confused. Yet in all his bewilderment he clung to one idea.

"I love the Lord Jesus Christ," Helen Powell heard him say repeatedly.

"That is only right," his tormentors conceded; "we shall all respect you for that. Only give up the idea of breaking caste."

"I love the Lord Jesus Christ," he insisted. However harassed and exhausted, he held fast to this certainty of his soul.

"Yes, yes, certainly; but keep your caste; just promise not to break it," worried the others.

Still he would not yield. Then they sent for the mother. She came in, wailing loudly, and stood before her son beating her breast and tearing at her hair, in between uttering shrieks of woe, while the enemies crowded round urging him to end her distress by the simple promise to serve Christ in private only. The scene became intolerable.

"Yes, all right, I will do that," said Nanjandappa, overborne at last; "take her home."

Helen Powell had tried in vain to secure free choice for the assaulted spirit and mind. She attempted one last rescue.

"Are you really satisfied with that arrangement?" she asked him.

"Yes," he said dejectedly. But it was manifest that he had been browbeaten into consent.

"It is all right," the caste men jubilated hurriedly, "he has agreed to serve Christ privately only. You need not trouble to talk to him any more."

A few days afterwards she managed to see him privately.

"Are you really resolved to give up baptism?" she asked.

"Oh no," he replied, rather to her astonishment.

"But you told them you would," she said wonderingly.

"I only said it," he answered.

Without meaning it, apparently, and seemed to think it quite justifiable.

The others also seemed to know what to expect, and that

promises might not count for much. During the days that followed, Helen Powell found that interviews became increasingly difficult to arrange. She exchanged letters with Nanjandappa. Later on a member of a wealthy Brahmin family himself told her that all her letters to Nanjandappa and his to her were opened and read. "We read them all before the addressees did."

He felt, apparently, no shame or even qualms about it; confessed calmly to having been an accessory himself, and seemed pleased with their cleverness in managing to get hold of the letters. These things are possible in India. The deplorable lack of moral feeling and of public standards to which they point may be guessed by the thoughtful reader. When Indians are earthly-minded—for instance, when attacked in caste feeling or when bent on material success or profit—there are few lengths to which they will not go. And at the same time it is true that when spiritually minded, Indians will go greater lengths than most other races in the world.

Here in Penuroy it was the worse side of India that was turned towards Nanjandappa's struggling spirit. Illogically, others were made to suffer also. Helen Powell, who had never in the least tried to influence Nanjandappa to be a Christian (though she had certainly demanded fair play for him), found herself boycotted. Her daily sewing-class for Hindu girls collapsed; not a child came near her house. Rangavachari had, if anything, tried to persuade the man to remain within the fold of Hinduism—yet he was included in the boycott. He was known to be a reformer and no respecter of caste—that sufficed. A Christian doctor's widow, living at Penuroy, had never had any dealings with Nanjandappa, but simply because she was a Christian of good standing they ostracized her also; angry, perhaps, with the final defeat which overtook them.

For succour must have come to Nanjandappa's beleaguered soul. A few weeks later he took leave from his post at Penuroy, travelled secretly to a town a hundred and twenty miles distant and there received baptism. For a time he remained with his new friends.

Had the wounds inflicted on his spirit been so deep that he emerged from the struggle like another pilgrim of old, lame in part of his nature? Or had he, perhaps, expected everyone in his new circle to be an exact replica of Christ, and of his conception of Christ as the Lord of unfailing understanding and patience and love? Alas for human nature! It takes most of us a lifetime to learn to recognize God in the tiny and infinitely partial reflection of Him which is all that any single human personality can reveal of Him. Nanjandappa looked for complete ideals, which were to be shaped, moreover, in Indian mode and thought. And those were not yet the days when Indian religious thought was appreciated by many Christian workers. Indian atmosphere and development had not come to be considered, as they are now, not only desirable, but right and necessary, in the Christian Church. Rifts appeared. He withdrew from his associates and returned to his teacher's work when his leave was up. He never formally joined any Christian church, though he continued to call himself a Christian. His was a nature that craved for human companionship; yet throughout his life he remained a solitary.

The friendlessness of those days must have been hard for him to bear. His mother, of course, would no longer live with him, he had no one to look after him. From his letters to Helen Powell, who has very kindly allowed me to use them, the further story of his life, and of the circumstances in which it was lived, may be told.

"I have some friends here who mock me and tell others near them when I get up to go that I am a fool and an outcaste. For bathing I have to go to the other side of the river, a mile and a half from here; there I can bathe and wash my clothes without being objected to." (One gathers the *dhobi* refused to wash for a man who had broken his caste.) "It is difficult to get water for drinking and for washing my feet when soiled by walking in the street after rain."

In his work at school he met similar trials.

"People here will not forget my great sin of breaking caste. Many parents want to remove me from the school for fear of their sons being spoiled through my irreligious mode of life. Many of the boys in school show me that other teachers are more worthy of respect, that I do not deserve any. This is because parents speak ill of me; when the father of a student wants to ask about his son's progress and behaviour he goes to another teacher, although the boy is in my class. Pandit Raghavendra told all Brahmins in the town that I would spoil the caste of all the boys. After a time he found out he was wrong in this idea, and even began to like some of my views. May God teach him that I am his friend."

His young Hindu wife was permanently withheld from him and considered to be a widow. Several times he tried to see her, but on each occasion was stoned out of the village. At length his loneliness and domestic hardships made him think of remarriage. But his unwillingness to be a recognized member of any mission or church created difficulties in obtaining a Christian wife. Ultimately he found an orphan, a Hindu girl, whom he married by Brahmo rites. Jaya proved a good and faithful companion to him, but she remained a Hindu and brought up their children as such. No doubt she felt the need of belonging *some*where.

For Nanjandappa it meant that in his own home, in the intimate relationships of life as husband and father, he remained alone.

The old mother paid occasional visits after the marriage; but in no conciliatory spirit.

"My wife is afraid of my mother. When she comes here she tells all loudly that I am a pariah, that my wife is a low-caste girl, that I am spoiled in all respects and do not deserve love from anyone. I try to pacify her in vain. . . . This day from four o'clock till six my wife and my mother were quarrelling and abusing. I could not do anything but ask Jaya to keep quiet. For this, she began to weep and wept the whole night, saying that because she had none to help her among her caste people my mother treats her so badly. She even cursed Annapurna and her mother for deceiving her when they praised me to her before our marriage. She talks like that because she is young and has little experience. I could not blame her, or request my mother to be quiet, knowing well she would be worse if I only raised my voice. Silence would bring peace sooner; otherwise I might have made my poor angry mother do serious things."

But in these trials inner solace did not fail. Many and constant are the expressions of fervent love and devotion to the Lord Jesus Christ.

"The Sub-Registrar here gave me a book, *Christ—a Myth*, by Takur K. C. Varna. It brings historical evidence to show that there was a man called Jesus who was wicked and was killed. I tell it briefly. The Sub-Registrar asked me how I liked it. I said although it was proved that Jesus was not born it mattered not to me. The life of Jesus according to the Gospels does more to help me than many such books as Takur's. Even if all men believe that Jesus was not born it is good for me to believe He lived and is working now. I cannot dispute about His divinity. I am satisfied above measure with the life of the Lord Jesus. If any man once sees the heart of Jesus he is sure to love it and to follow Him. If once anybody feels the love of Jesus he is surely a new man. I am fresh and happy when Jesus is with me. I am sorrowful and weak when I forget Him. . . . All my power is His. I give my heart to Jesus. I fly to Him. I know how my Lord Jesus told and is telling me that He is my Relation and Friend."

In that school of friendship and intimacy he learnt to notice many things and to think fresh thoughts.

"I get a few things, or fruit, for my children. When I give these to my children I see another child, of my neighbour, or strangers, looking at me. My heart tells me I should make that child understand somehow that I am not defrauding it by not letting it share equally with my children, or not letting it have as much freedom as it likes in my house. I feel this is cruel. What is the state of that other child's mind, caused by my unkind and selfish act in the distribution of eatables and fruit?"

The Western Christian would think the solution an easy one. Is it by a slow path of painful reflection, such as Nanjandappa's, that the deep-rooted idea of putting the family—all relations, not only children—first and foremost has to be widened; or, to use modern jargon, sublimated?

He was always conscious of the difficulty of really knowing any human being, and the risk of judging.

"I am not able to understand all about anybody without seeing all the ways of a person for a long time, and even then there will be something left unseen. But it seems to me that in this twentieth century my Hindu brothers forget their duty to their country and only talk about the greatness, nobility, justice, and wisdom of their ancients. Very few educated brothers are working for the country, though we need many more men to work in the direction of reform. . . . Some do. K. Siva Rama is the Brahmin Karnam of Konagiri. He told me he always addresses a low-caste man as '*ayya*,' or '*appa*,' and said it was sinful to call him 'ho thou,'[1] 'thou what,'[2] or, 'donkey,' when they so humbly address a Brahmin as Lord, Divinity, Wisdom, etc. He is trying to remove this evil from our country."

Caste and superstition troubled him much. "Our former head master wanted me to believe that the skin of a Brahmin is more sacred than the whole body of a Sudra, though the Sudra in moral respects was equal to, or greater than, the

[1] Telugu: oray! [2] Yemi ra!

Brahmin. . . . Our present head master told me that if he were to occupy any house facing West there would be a death in his house, as the star of his name did not harmonize with houses facing West. He was angry with me when I said why not change his name and go free of this fear all his life. Such superstitions are excusable in the ignorant, but not in the educated."

Nanjandappa had cause for being troubled on this score. To see how strong a hold superstition still has at the present hour on educated people one need only open the advertisement pages of the daily or weekly Indian Press. The charms, medicines, amulets, lucky stones—promising success in exams., fortune in business, healthy sons, immunity from disease, etc.—and the testimonials of B.A.s and M.A.s and high officials to their efficacy, might surprise a modern reader. Yet advertisers and vendors of these wares must know their public.

But the other side is always there too. The same letter contains cheering information, though the epidemic raging when he wrote was terrible enough.

"Plague is increasing in the sheds to which the people have been moved from the town. The eldest son of a teacher died this morning; the father came to me and wept bitterly. . . . When I was going into the town I saw a merchant, gone mad, he had fever and a *bubo* on his thigh. Some merchants were arranging to give him food. I went to see his state this evening. He is left under a tree. On every side death is seen, and terror. But there was a Brahmin, the Revenue Inspector. He had the courage and kindness to touch and to place two dead persons in his cart, an old woman and a young girl, and drive it himself to the funeral place. This was at the beginning of the outbreak. His goodness moved me much.

"Before this, when there was cholera in the town and a police constable died of cholera and no one had the courage to touch the corpse, this Revenue Inspector removed it in his own cart, driving himself. What a splendid man. Then his own son, a student in the high school, died of plague, and now this truly good man has died himself also."

Alas, that this picture of "a truly good man" (and only those who know India can gauge *how* good—touching a corpse means long defilement, besides the risk of infection) should immediately be followed by another. The people who had been turned out of their houses were to be allowed back when the epidemic subsided, after disinfection and white-washing of the walls.

"The Sanitary Inspector here, a Brahmin, a relation of the Union Clerk, took four annas from every poor man after the whitewashing, though this was done by the owners, and he only then marked it D. The ignorant people did not understand that there was no need for payment, but they were afraid to question him. Some did not pay and waited for the order of the Sub-Collector. There was no order; for people can re-occupy their houses freely after whitewashing them. Now the Sub-Collector is back the Sanitary Officer is afraid and is marking houses without demanding anything. But a poor washerwoman told my wife she had agreed to wash the Sanitary Inspector's clothes gratis for some months."

Again and again there are references to caste and corruption in public services in his letters, and pitiful stories told of victims without power or ability to reach justice "through the proper channel." In his own department of Education he sometimes wellnigh despaired, and came to the depressing conclusion "that it is wiser to get an appointment by payment" (i.e. bribe) "than go on suffering, as people want only money and do not care for justice. What is the good of my being against this—things are going on in this way without any check."

His longing to imitate Christ, the great Lover of men, in service to his own kind could not find satisfying outlets. As the years passed, his eyes became opened to another suffering going on in his country, that of animals. His sympathy and indignation were roused by the slaughter that takes place at many religious festivals, often under circumstances of great cruelty. He joined a League working on Indian lines of the S.P.C.A. and fared forth on the new pilgrim way of combating these practices, chiefly in the long hot weather holidays.

His letters describing his experiences on these occasions reveal a side of Hinduism not generally so well known, perhaps not guessed at by readers of, for instance, Tagore's books, or Sarojini Naidu's poetry, or such exquisite biographies as that of Sarok Nalini Dutt, by her husband. These books, the ideas they contain, and the lives to which they witness, are all facts and true parts of India, the significance of which cannot be overrated. But there are other parts and other facts. The wild and lawless qualities inherent in tribes and races who came to India long ago as conquerors have not disappeared from their descendants; "the mild and gentle Hindu" is a truth, but a partial one, and must not blind us to the presence of fierceness, excitability, the possibility of breaking all bounds, not least at religious festivals.

"At Yemanur there is a great yearly festival. A Mohammedan saint is buried there. On his grave is a brass or gold ornament, called the *parlu*; below it is a bull, like one in Siva's temples. On either side of the bull stands a row of shining brass horses, kept generally in a house or temple." (The festival would appear to be a curious mixture of Hinduism and Mohammedanism. The saint would probably be worshipped first by Mohammedans; but Hindus are never averse to adding to their Pantheon, and always pleased to increase their festive occasions.[1])

"Yemanur is a small village with only few houses; but for the *Jatra* (festival) persons of all castes and from many parts go there with goats and sheep to kill, and to feed

[1] See *Pirlu* festival, Chap. i.

Mohammedan fakirs and Hindu brothers. In a small rivulet that has only little and dirty water, males and females bathe and then go to the temple with goats and sheep and sugar. The rush is so great that a man like myself is afraid to go, as one cannot reach the temple without pushing and rudely handling other brothers and sisters. The number is about 300,000; the animals may number about forty or fifty thousand. It is said that people with venereal diseases go there to be cured, or women desiring children, all with goats to kill. Hindus buy them sometimes, instead of bringing them, and give them to Mohammedans to kill and eat, to please the Saint of Yemanur. Sometimes 24,000 animals are butchered.

"An area of ten miles is full of men and women and animals. Wherever one looks one sees goats, people, and carts. We could see the dead bodies of animals hung on carts, on both sides. The scenes are very awkward, pitiful, and barbarous.

"On the last day they sometimes carry portions in bags and clothes to their homes. In the trains it is difficult to bear the stench of rotting meat. Sometimes kids and lambs only a few days old are brought for slaughter. Animals are sometimes left in the terribly hot sun for four or five days without anything to eat or drink. We brought this to the notice of the municipality. Also we sent an appeal to Government and municipal councils to prohibit carcases being hung on trees and on carts in the camp.

"The gathering of such an assembly looked like a dream to me. There were shops of all kinds, plays, dramas, circuses, cinemas, sweetmeats, glassware, pottery, hardware, carved boxes and door-frames, books, pictures, fruit, also hotels, and coffee, tea, and food shops, as in a large city . . . at times I thought I was in a city like Hyderabad.

"Our League had sent helpers. Fifteen rich Jains from Bijapur, thirty-five from Hubli, six from Gadag, along with our branch, were present; all of us eager to lessen the slaughter by praying the people, by preaching, by distributing tracts, by telling them they should worship God and saints with flowers, fruit, and sweets, and make the place holy instead of polluting it by beheading poor creatures which would curse mankind at the time of their death.

"Many volunteers worked with us also. From 9 a.m. to 12 we visited places where herds were kept. Some of the preachers were very rich men, and very aged, 60 or 65 years of age; yet they worked better than some younger ones. They walked in the hot sun, scorched by it, thirsty, always humble. They only prayed people, requested, begged, fell at the feet of those who had bought sheep for killing, asking them to substitute sweet-smelling and fragrant things; to feed the poor, to clothe the naked, to help the widow, and give water to the thirsty. Some animals were bought by these rich gentlemen. Some people who intended to purchase for sacrifice went away without buying, convinced by us; some, on our urging, returned the animals already bought. Some wept when I spoke of the animals' pains of death, some fell at my feet, being thankful to have learnt a better way of worship. Wherever brothers did not yield to our entreaties brothers of our party used to run to the place where I was at work and take me over to these others to pray and plead on behalf of the poor beasts. I had the chance of speaking at nearly two hundred places within fifteen hours.

"We were not sufficient workers; we were nearly seventy, but for such a huge assembly we needed five hundred workers and five hundred volunteers. I am sorry we did not succeed in saving all animals, but we saved some thousands. My body was boiled, my feet burnt, my eyes were burning, my whole body painful, going about the camp in the hot sun, preaching and falling at the feet of brothers. The work was too much, now I am not able to talk, not able to walk, no, nor to explain, nor to think of what to do next—I must take rest for a few days. . . ."

"I am going to tell you about things here. It is *Poundarika Yagna.*" (*Yagna*, sacrifice.) "A *Smartha* Brahmin gentleman of this place has been trying to perform this sacrifice in which forty goats will be killed and much money will be spent to feed Brahmin brothers only. In addition to the goats it is said a man also must be killed in this *Yagna*. As the Government does not allow this they are going to . . ." (here followed the description of a rite that cannot be reproduced in print.) "This is considered to be equal to the killing of a man. You may thereby consider the civilization of my Hindu brothers. . . ."

"At the Devangiri *Jatra* 3,000 sheep and 30 buffaloes were to be killed before the temple of Durga Devi, goddess of all the people of that place. Several Jains, Lingaits, and Vaisyas helped in trying to stop the butchery, also the Police Inspector and Tahsildar. After the buffalo for the goddess was killed food was mixed with its blood and thrown around the town. There was much fear whether peace could be kept. Often people get drunk and reckless, then run in mobs, throwing food about, also killing kids or lambs. Nine different places were assigned to the purpose of killing. Some of our helpers went with the mob; some stood at the killing-places and saved many animals, by paying money, and by having coconuts broken as offerings instead; nearly five hundred coconuts were broken. But at the last place some person suddenly threw a helpless kid among the crowd, their leader killed it by cutting it at the waist into two pieces; then he threw the pieces in the air, where they fell again on the assembled people. After this the persons who had promised to help maintain peace lost hope; they said they could not control the youths now. But then the police helped by arresting persons drunk and breaking the peace. Everything went well after all; a few goats were killed in secret, but not thousands as in other years. This is a wonderful result. It is said that once in two years blood used to flow in the gutter like water, and that drunkenness was terrible.

"At Secunderabad on the 15th and 16th July, 1922, there was *Devi Puja*." (*Devi*, goddess; *Puja*, worship.) "People of all castes dress in their best, and, adorned with jewels, go to the temple, with turmeric, incense, fruits, flowers, and a pot of water smeared with saffron, leaves of margosa tied to it. A servant drags a goat or sheep by a string, it follows them bleating. It is to be killed and given to a Sudra brother, if the giver is a Vaisya or other high-caste man.

"Hundreds, even thousands, are killed then. The streets are full of drops of blood, the clothes of many people are smirched with blood-marks. Some rich ladies pay two or three *pice* to sit on the tops of houses near" (flat roofs are referred to) "to see these scenes of death. Men and women push each other rudely in the crowd. The killing begins at 5 or 6 a.m. on Sunday and closes at 2 p.m. on Monday. For more than thirty hours it goes on. The butchers are often drunk; sometimes they miss their aim and cause much suffering to the animals by not killing in one stroke. They get tired, too, and are slow to end their pain. I saw no one pitying them. Almost all believe the goddess wants the blood of the poor things.

"Buffaloes are killed also. At 3 a.m. one of the fearful and wild men stands before the temple. He is called *Potu Raj*" (buffalo king). "A man throws a little goat at him; he tears it to pieces at the throat, and sucks its blood. Then he goes round the temple with fearful cries, wild and inhuman, with the entrails of the goat hung round his neck. His hand is seen raised, smeared with blood. At 4 a.m. the buffalo is killed. It takes three or four strokes till the neck is cut. A deep pit is dug for the blood to drain into, and it overflows the pit, too. I am trying to show you the scene—I am not exaggerating. I went there on the night of Saturday and returned on Monday. We had worked there for a month beforehand, with singing and preaching and teaching. I am glad to tell you that the number of animals killed was a little less than before.

"But I felt so troubled that I could not take meals or drink water for forty-three hours. I prayed and fasted, and tried to understand the thing. I forgot food as I thought of the animals. Nor did I feel tired, though I was walking in the streets and speaking to hundreds of brethren about the unnecessary pain and killing. In the month of preparation I used to get up at 3 a.m., then bathe and dress and short prayer till 4.30, then out in the streets till 7.30, then home and read Bhagavat Gita, Bible, *Little Garden of Roses*, by Thomas à Kempis; out again for preaching till midday, or till one or two o'clock, as the work pressed; a short rest and again to work in the afternoon and evening. I do not know how I managed, hunger and fatigue are not felt by me, except now and then. I don't use shoes, I have not for fifteen years. I feel as if I were treading on and destroying an animal for my comfort; I don't object to others wearing them, but I don't wear them myself. As I walked so much my heels became broken. I had to walk on tip-toe for two or three days till they healed again."

Throughout the ages the history of religions shows strange conceptions of God being served in wild and bloody scenes. But that they should still exist in India to-day may come as a surprise to the readers of these extracts from letters written by a son of India. If it is not an impertinence one would like to add that surely they come as a call to educated India to help their less-instructed brethren to possess their heritage of *bhakti* without excesses that must be revolting to their own highest conceptions and aspirations.

The devotion and zeal of Nanjandappa and his helpers

shine out the more radiantly against such a background. India comes second to none in the capacity of many of her children for self-sacrifice. Indeed, it is a question whether the really significant facts in these scenes are, not the ignorant, unrestrained and fanatical crowds, but the little groups of devoted workers of various creeds, all sons of India, striving for enlightenment and progress and a better interpretation of God.

His strenuous labours wore out Nanjandappa's frail body. His health broke down. He died in 1929, in a Christian medical *Ashram* in the Tamil country, his longing to see the spirit of Christ exhibited without a flaw satisfied at last by the loving service of European and Indian doctors and nurses, in whose midst he passed to his rest.

Much obloquy and constant misunderstanding had been his throughout life. Both sides, Christians and non-Christians, thought him a crank. (In his later years he had joined the *Arya Samaj*. This *Samaj* is opposed to the idea of a personal God and denies Incarnation. Yet he still called himself a Christian. His state of mind illustrates afresh the curious Indian capacity of harbouring mutually excluding tenets.) Yet while criticizing and objecting the world around him had been silently impressed by his loving and gentle spirit, as well as by his labours.

"Him whom they had despised and oppressed all his life they now found they held in high regard," wrote his widow. The townpeople came when they heard of his death and carried out the funeral obsequies. They held a public meeting presided over by the Tahsildar, and in honour of his memory raised a sum to relieve the widow by paying off the mortgage on his house. They subscribed two hundred and fifty rupees on the spot, one man alone giving a hundred rupees. A testimony, indeed, to the impression made on them by this loving and selfless follower of Christ, exhibiting as far as in him lay the truth of his own words: "If any man once sees the heart of Jesus he is sure to love it and to follow Him. If once anybody feels the love of Jesus he is surely a new man."

1 And perhaps in other ways there was more fruit in that devoted life than was seen while he was still here.

In September 1930 a letter from a Christian teacher, working in the same town and in the very school where Nanjandappa taught, reached me. The writer says, "We are twelve teachers on the staff. Eleven are Brahmins. I am the only Christian. But there is no difference, they are all friendly with me and treat me with courtesy. No unkind word is said to me on account of my being a Christian."

My correspondent is a "born" Christian, and therefore gave no offence to caste loyalties by breaking them, as Nanjandappa had done. On the other hand, his origin would be presumed to be low caste, thus carrying its own stigma. Yet he is respected and liked. Nanjandappa's faithful fight in that school has not failed to make the uphill way less steep for his successor.

CHAPTER XIX

IN SCHOOLS AND STREETS

FROM the verandah of the Ramidi rest-house I look out on deep midsummer. Showers have refreshed the land; little yellow and blue flowers show confiding faces amongst the vivid green of the grass. Thorn-trees are covered with golden bloom, amid which the wild pigeons coo an interminable concert; the tree shadows lie on the ground like tranquil pools of darkness. Beyond the hedges of prickly-pear fields are being ploughed; extra yoke of oxen are tinkling along the road towards the aid of their brothers stolidly tramping the furrows; faint and purple the Taramulla hills show in the distance.

While writing, a war is being waged against innumerable flies; bang! the fly-flap has killed or stunned one; it is swept on to the ground, where big soldier-ants are swarming; in a second one of them drags it away. But all is not plain sailing, a bigger and stronger ant comes along, there are arguments about that fly. The smaller ant goes off empty antennæ-ed—or whatever it is that ants drag with. "It is a bad, bad world," as the worm said when only half of it got away; the fat *minah* bird hopping about the grass picking, and looking anything but miserable, is responsible for this remark, which, I believe, is not original. Perish the people who said things before us!

While the years are bringing the philosophic mind (let us hope, though the above tag hardly illustrates it!) they are taking away, unkindly, an amenable body. It is well work here was started years ago; I do not think I could now hop about Ramidi like an energetic frog seeking some convenient water-spout to creep into.[1] Luckily the frog has arrived in a pond. After the hot midday journey yesterday a

[1] See *An Uphill Road in India*, Chaps. ix and x.

chair was ready in the market; all one had to do was to sit there like a Buddha. Peter, the energetic head master, had levied entrance fees to the school sports; the *pice* thus collected mounted up sufficiently to buy prizes for winners, betel-nuts for the town magnates, sweets for both schools, and hire a band to charm our savage breasts. Jumping and racing boys, surrounded by a trampling multitude, excited the sand and dust, always flying round plentifully in Ramidi, to a pitch of activity difficult to swallow; but it was for yet other reasons than grit and glare that I was glad of my dark glasses. Ramidi holds many memories. . . .

One more was added to these last night when the successful public proceedings were followed by a quiet talk in the moonlight with the Christian teachers. The thought that it is not the outward things that constitute the real progress, that the true coming of the Kingdom is ever an inward one, had been our theme. That inward coming is ever a far more difficult one than the establishment of any outward organization. Peter is experiencing the way of the Cross in unexpected quarters, although so successful with his school and the non-Christian citizens of Ramidi who regard him as a man of importance and a refuge in their troubles, as well as arbitrator in their quarrels. But he is of partly Tamil origin, and this is the Telugu country. His Christian fellow-workers throughout the district are all Telugus. Old tribal traditions and instincts, operative throughout human history everywhere, but here in India with particularly unabated force, are at work. Envy, suspicion, jealousy, whisperings, slanders, follow. The Tamil people possess noted qualities of leadership; the Telugus and Kanarese are more gentle and friendly, but rarely leaders. Tamilians resident amongst them generally come to the front. They may be gifted and well-intentioned and in every way suitable for prominent posts, but the attitude of Telugu and Kanarese workers in the Church and in the Mission remains unfriendly.

"Why should we have this foreigner to rule over us?" For though resident amongst them for a generation and heartily identifying themselves with all local interests, they are still classed as "foreigners." Tamils (18,750,000), Telugus (29,500,000), Kanarese (10,250,000), are all of the same Dravidian stock; yet the divisions among them are sharp, and unwillingness to mingle smoulders. How many still are the uphill steps India (aye, and the Christian Church!) has to take before the vision of the Greatest of Asiatics, "*that they all may be one*," can be fulfilled?

So poor Peter has his trials, and I don't suppose he is a complete saint yet himself, though his fellow-workers are offering him a good chance of graduating. And indeed he is making use of some, though with a Hindu neighbour this time. One uphill step, anyway. He was telling me a little shyly: "I had a grudge against my neighbours. They had made a drain for their dirty water into my courtyard. I complained. There was to be a case about it. Meanwhile I stopped the drain. They were angry.

"The missionary came here and announced a Communion Service. On my way to it I thought of my neighbours. I ran back; with my own hands I pulled the plug out of the drain and said to my neighbours: 'Let us live at peace.' They were utterly amazed; they fell down before me and tried to catch my hands, but I ran away again and came to the service and received the Communion."

> "From heart to heart it sinks, it steals, it flows,
> From these that know Thee still infecting those."[1]

Even when they know only a very little. In the girls' school this morning I was told of the death of a schoolgirl but a few days ago. She had been the joy and idol of the poor grandmother and aunts (her only relations), who broke out into the customary loud wailing as I entered their home.

[1] George Macdonald, *Diary of an Old Soul.*

Presently they grew quieter; neighbours crowded in. "We never saw such a death," said one; "we have seen great ones die, but not like this girl." "She prayed," added another, "she said golden words." Gladly would I have heard more details; but direct questions seemed too clumsy a touch; with deepened interest I listened later to the lyrics and Bible stories her class-fellows knew; these, and what she learned in daily school prayers, had been the staff which sustained the dying child and so profoundly impressed neighbours.

Constantly it is borne in upon me that it is work among the young that is the most urgent and the most promising. But the battles this entails are legion; the irregularity of the pupils in these rural parts is a minor one; the most wearing is the one with teachers. Here in Ramidi a young Brahmin is acting in place of a sick teacher. His great idea is to whack the pupils into silence and immobility. I took his stick from him, but I had to leave him his hands. Smack! a resounding blow—during inspection. I drew the Inspector's attentions to it that he might reprove the Brahmin more impressively than I. He did; but habits are strong, and smacks punctuated the inspection. The Inspector came to his class and with his usual patience began to elicit. He is one of the few Indians I have met who possess the gift of humour. It carried him a long way with the children, who enjoyed his examination thoroughly.

In this class a pupil was very slow. The slowest should have been able to follow, but she was lazy as well. "This is the time for hitting her," I advised gravely; "manifestly you cannot get on without." The Inspector, with his quick sense of fun, went off into fits of laughter. The teacher, who has not an ounce of humour, looked at me scandalized. How could I be so contradictory; telling him, the teacher, not to smack but advising the Inspector to do it? The white people could not be relied on; but he, a Brahmin, would help the Brahmin Inspector! The latter, by a most patient process, was arriving at his end; the elucidation and use of the word *imitate.* He had elicited that when monkeys do so and so they were imitating, and now asked: "When we see someone run and begin to run ourselves, what are we doing?" "We are imitating," cried the helpful teacher precipitately, and could not understand why the Inspector and I looked at him speechlessly, while the whole class parroted in the old hopeless style, "We are imitating, we are imitating."

Later on the Inspector gave model lessons, in which his tireless enthusiasm and unfailing patience won my whole admiration. When one meets such genuine devotion to work and unsparing efforts to make it a success I want to shout with the best "India for the Indians!" But, for my sins, I meet it only rarely.

Yet the fact that one does meet it is surely significant. Selfless zeal and self-denial are not anywhere common characteristics of the masses; but if they exist at all, even in a few, will the few not act as leaven to their nation?

Then these reflections of hope get damped again.

To Ramidi came the news of the ever-threatening volcano at Bukkuru becoming active once more. School troubles in that place (or indeed, in any other) never cease. This time it was a flare-up among the Mohammedans. Some time before they had fallen out amongst themselves; the rival factions could no longer worship God together; a separate prayer wall had been put up by the seceding minority. But quarrelling is not conducive to anybody's spirit of worship; the religion of the whole community degenerated; all was neglected to such an extent that even the mosque was left uncared for and became in danger of falling to pieces. To repair their piety they got hold of a kind of Mohammedan missionary. This man, very wisely and properly, thought that addressing himself to the young would be a good way of building their Mecca again. A number of young were conveniently assembled in the Mission girls' school; wherefore he announced that he would open a girls' school and proceeded to order the people to send their children to him. The people obeyed their attractive new broom. The news that arrived was that the flourishing Mission school was practically empty. At a day's notice I was off to Bukkuru.

On arrival there six or seven of my old Mohammedan friends came for a council. It appeared that though all Mohammedan factions united in loving the new man they had their doubts about supporting him. A genius suggested that he be employed in the Mission school. That would at one stroke solve the difficulty of his support and the problem of rival schools, and, further, ensure that their daughters would be taught exactly according to their ideas. They urged the merits of this proposal upon me.

"Hm, hm," I said meditatively. "If you Mohammedans are all so keen on him do you mean you cannot support him without the aid of the Christian Mission?"

Irony was lost on them. "We are so poor," they replied.

"Yes, you are poor, but as poor as all that? Don't you think you might feed him for three months at all events? You quarrel a bit here now and then, don't you? Three years ago you all swore by Mullah Sahib—none of you want him now; he had to leave this place. You had one prayer wall; now you have to have a second one, because of dissensions. I should like to see how you get on with this man."

"Oh, but we all like *him*; he will teach us prayer and to be at peace."

"I am very glad to hear it," I said. "Shall we go and see him?"

We repaired to his house. There was the man, sitting surrounded by my girls, who greeted me smilingly. After proper preliminaries we reached the matter in hand. Was it, I hinted, a good way of re-establishing peace and righteousness to introduce a fresh bone of contention, and bring confusion and doubt where to send their children among families here?

He seemed not unwilling to be persuaded—and quite manifestly eager to enter Mission service. Was there a faint distrust of his co-religionists? "I would double the strength of your school," he sought to bribe me.

"Would you?" I replied. "Then here is an offer. Send all our girls back; start afresh with new girls, and when you have as strong a school as ours was before you upset it we will talk again."

As he did not seem very willing to forgo his vantage ground of present possession the adults were advised to convene a meeting to decide finally which school they would support. At the discussion some said, "We will send to the Mission school." Some others: "We will send to the new man." Most: "We will do what everybody else does."

The real sufferers were the poor children. I was visiting in their homes till evening. A fourth-standard girl slipped into the room in the dark from a neighbouring house. She was trembling so that I thought she was ill. "Are you not well, Rahim Bi?"

"Quite well," she stammered. It dawned on me then she was only very excited and even near hysterics, just for the pleasure of the meeting and the hope of getting back to her old school.

"I want to come back," she whispered. "Lots of the girls cry when they have to go to the new school. But I am *gosha* now, they won't let me go out at all."

"You shall have a covered cart," I promised, "then you may. I will try and get you a scholarship, that will pay for the cart."

She came to school next day, all tremulous eagerness, and cried with joy to be back.

My heart went out to her in pity. Those first months

and years of being shut up in little back rooms and backyards, what suffering they must mean to young and eager girls! Till then they have roamed the streets freely. Then comes a day when they may go out no more. I thought of a girl very dear to me, in England, about as old as Rahim Bi. If she had to be shut up now, if all that vividness and brightness, all that eager questioning, the developing of mind and soul, all the awakening interests, the shy feelers put forth into life, the dawning affections—now had the door slammed in their face: "keep *gosha.*" It is unthinkable.

As the Moslems of Bukkuru could not reach a unanimous conclusion the Mission school was kept on with eleven faithful ones. If anyone finds life boring at home let them start managing schools in our Telugu country!

The reader shall not have the thrills of anxiety that fell to the manager's lot—with inspection imminent—but hear the end now. Within six months the people had quarrelled with the new man. Most pupils dribbled back to the Mission school. Before the year was out the Mohammedan teacher had closed his anæmic school and sent his own daughter to ours, with a written request to receive her and to bring her on well!

But for the time being all was in "doubt, hesitation, and pain," and besides this little mountain of perplexity caused by this school, sundry other little hillocks kept cropping up, one being my own refractory "Brother Ass." On the hurried journey to Bukkuru (which is thirteen miles from the nearest railway station) I had been caught in a storm; the bullocks —perhaps to escape the drenching rain—were running furiously; jolt, jolt, over stones and ruts; then suddenly, flop, plop, the cart lurched violently and fell on its side. One of the two wheels had come off. Recovered from the bump, I adjusted myself to the preposterous slant and peered for rescue through a landscape white with rain, and feeling drips on my neck through the bamboo cover. The driver took it as philosophically as I; at length another cart passed and its inmates helped us back into equilibrium. A twig from a bush near by furnished a new wheel pin, of about the same security as the one which had caused the accident. The further consequence was a disturbed internal economy: "Have you been caught by a chill?" said the Bukkuru dresser sympathetically when I asked for medicine. It seemed a much more sensible way of putting it than our usual formula.

The journey back to Andapur over those jolty thirteen miles loomed a little threateningly. The night before departure Erana slept in the verandah, as the kitchen roof had fallen in during the rain.

His coughing made sleep shyer than ever; in despair I sent him off to lie in the cart standing under the trees, ready for early departure. But now the rats began. Erana was recalled to take the bread-tin into the cart. Being deprived of this, the rats retaliated by starting on my cot. At two o'clock the second cart-man drove up, the bells round the bulls' necks tinkling cheerfully.

"Oh, cart-driver! tie up the animals beyond the gate!"

"I will not."

"Why not?"

"The devil is outside."

To me it seemed he was just as much inside. Towards dawn I slept; rather too late for the intended five o'clock start. But by fine scurrying and reckless driving and jolting, we caught the one and only day train. After arrival at home, however, I collapsed afresh—pain racked me. The pitiableness of the spectacle of a preaching, admonishing, criticizing parsoness reduced to faintest whispers for days on end, moved me to inextinguishable laughter inside; it was so refined a discipline!

At night Dorcas turned the bath-room into a witch's den. On a charcoal fire glowed a seething cauldron where mysterious leaves were brewing; when she strewed in dry powders a weird steam arose; smells too, I presume, though I could perceive none; the *finale* was a live charcoal thrown in, when the whole hissed up in proper satanic fashion. I huddled over the sizzling mass, with a blanket over it and me, and felt as if I were somebody's supper, cooking to perfection. "Are you perspiring?" asked Dorcas unnecessarily. "Floods," I mumbled. "Wipe dry," she commanded, and I obeyed; whereupon she introduced more powder, more charcoal fizzle, and I dived under the blanket again. After several repetitions she decreed it was enough. "Oh, not enough," I pleaded, ogling the warm glow lovingly, for the direct heat kept the pain in abeyance. However, the turn for the better came in due course, and daily life had me in its grip again.

After Bukkuru Mohammedans it was Brahmins at Dharmpalli. As I sat in the school there a little late-comer arrived and announced *meila*, i.e. unclean, defiled. The other children took it calmly, but were careful to keep away from Nursamma. Sonamma, who had not heard and sat down on the same bench, was decreed by them to be *meila* also.

"Why are you unclean?" I asked Nursamma.

"My elder sister died yesterday, in our house."

"What, Venkata Lakshmi?"

"Yes."

Venkata Lakshmi was an old schoolgirl. She had come home for her first confinement. I learned since that she was practically starved. Many Brahmins, and others also, hold the notion that it is wise to give little or no food for two days after a baby's birth. As this girl showed alarming symptoms they kept on with this treatment; giving her instead—brandy. For it is another prevalent idea amongst them that brandy is a splendid English medicine which will cure anything and restore the weakest patient. So poor

Venkata Lakshmi's flickering lamp of life was stimulated to burn till it had burnt itself out. It made one feel as mad as one is sad.

One may guess at their reasoning. The English are strong, they drink brandy and such things; is it not a part of their religion to take daily a whisky and soda? [1] Is it their source of strength? What else is?

Not their religion. Apparently they have none. Indian eyes, keenly observant of daily habits and drawing conclusions from these, do not see the Englishman perform religious ceremonies. Then, if it is their strong drinks, why should not we have this benefit?

That Brahmin women, in a distant and backward place like Dharmpalli, themselves in no personal contact with Britishers, should have their homes subtly invaded by rumours of certain British habits, is a fact the pathos of which is beyond comment.

Western alcohol and Indian ignorance and bad nursing between them had killed this young life; it was little use now to adjudicate blame. But in the sorrowful happening of a few days later the West had no hand. A little Brahmin schoolgirl had fallen sick. I was told of it in school and went to see her, about ten o'clock. I found her people lived in a rented room which could only be approached through a front room inhabited by the landlord's family. When I knocked, a woman opened the door an inch and said: "We have bathed." She meant that they were unwilling to let me come through and thus risk defilement and the consequent trouble of having to bathe again before they could take their meal. "Come later," she added. Unfortunately all that after-

[1] This I heard asserted myself at a public meeting in Andapur. It is true that the chairman, a Mohammedan, put it aside at once, though but by the somewhat flippant rejoinder that when Christianity began there were no whiskies and sodas. There remains the fact that the first speaker had thought what he said. What body of opinion had taught him to think so?

noon and evening I had to be elsewhere; and no one had said the illness was serious. Next morning, to my consternation, I heard little Lalita had died.

They put the child in the street to die, in obedience to a custom. Their thought is that the spirit is freed more easily when the body is laid on the earth. But usually this would be a private courtyard. In this case a pitiful situation had arisen; for beside the force of custom there was other pressure on the troubled family. The Brahmin house-owners, afraid of the uncleanness caused by a death within their walls, said to the parents, "Go at once and find another house."

"How can you tell us to go when the child is so ill?" pleaded the poor parents. But that illness was just the reason; fear of the subsequent defilement and inconvenience, perhaps having to leave the house themselves, if a corpse were in it. So while the little daughter lay dying they continued to press the distracted parents to leave. They owned no courtyard in which to lay the child; they had but that one inner room, and no time to search for another; nor would any house have opened to them to take in a dying person. At such times the callousness of a caste rule—originally no doubt a healthy sanitary one—becomes apparent. In their distress and perplexity they carried the little one out into the public street and laid her on the ground. The poor sufferer was not too far gone to realize the change and its significance.

"Oh, you have put me out here! Must I die, then?" she said piteously. Evidently she was frightened. The end had come during the night. Though the street was full of the story,—of a rule more powerful than parental love stepping in and filling the last hours of the dying child with fear,—none questioned the rule.

One longed to have a house and courtyard in all towns of our district, where people could die in peace if they had no other refuge. Impossible, of course, and even if one had such a place and it became known that sick people might be brought there to die, no others would come near the Christian living in such a defiled and unauspicious spot. How shall we break through the bonds of caste and fear?

In a house of high-caste ladies—not Brahmins this time—I met another instance of the fear of defilement and the tradition of men making of no effect the laws of human kindness. I had been telling them the story of the wise men from the East; how they were not offended by the poverty of the family when at last they found the Babe; and had drawn a parallel between this and the fact of many in India being stumbled at Christianity receiving low-castes; calling it contemptuously the religion of outcastes; but how, in reality, this was its glory.

An old woman hobbled in; trembling with weakness, she slowly sat down on the ground; the effort of coming had apparently exhausted her. "I, too, wanted to hear," she gasped feebly.

It turned out she was in the same pitiable state as the woman in the Gospels who touched the hem of Christ's garment. Here, alas, was no virtue to heal her; I could only ask why she was allowed to walk in the street by herself when she had hardly the strength to stand; was there no one to look after her?

"That is an example of the things you have been saying," said the mistress of the house. "Who would look after her? When one is old and ill and useless one can just die, nobody minds. If they like to go out they can, if they fall down with weakness who will pick them up?" At the same time she herself looked with evident disfavour upon the poor woman who was defiling her house; though it will be reckoned to her for righteousness that she raised no protest against her coming in and even spoke to her quite gently. A relation was sent for who presently arrived and scoldingly took the frail old woman away; our hostess seemed astonished at the effort to instil a little tenderness: "Why all this trouble for her?"

Because of the memory of words infectious with love, "Daughter, be comforted," said by a Man in an Eastern country which held similar ideas about defilement as the people sitting around me at that moment. Will any but He create the new atmosphere needed in the East?

* * * * *

The days bring shadow and shine. I have just come back from a scene over which lay the shadow of death; yet a radiance shone through the darkness. A very dearly loved fellow-worker was near the end of her journey. I fear it is the imperfections of teachers which have most frequently found mention; but Ammuni's work in the Extension has never deserved anything but praise. She has been a steady, reliable worker always. Alas, two years ago tubercular symptoms appeared in her. Sent to the special Sanatorium she seemed to recover and returned, but had to be sent back again. A month ago she came back from there with malarial complications. Now she lies dying, and had asked for the Lord's Supper. It is from that last service that I have just returned. Under such circumstances it almost breaks one down. "I shall not drink of this cup . . . till I drink it anew in my Father's Kingdom." Ammuni was troubled by heart, in addition to all else. There was no ease for her anywhere; she had to be propped up in a sitting position; bed sores afflicted; legs and arms had swollen; yet she raised her weak voice to direct her little daughter to put the *topi* I was holding somewhere, and to tell the nurse to fetch a chair. Paget's phrase—"the courtesy of the dying"—flashed into my mind and almost overcame me. Indeed, the whole scene was too moving for description, to lie there, waiting for the door to open.

"You are not afraid, Ammuni?"

"No, not at all."

Her inward peace and calm communicated itself.

"Almost I envy you," I said, "you are so near such great happiness."—But most of the things said at such times are not for repetition. We were looking over the border together; the end was near.

Was she also looking back over difficult years? Her life has not been an easy one; she was an orphan; her marriage held many struggles and disappointments. But from her face shone only calm serenity; even about her child she was at peace. "I have committed her to God."

Outside the hot dry winds of March shook the last leaves from the banyan-trees; then they seemed to hush in their course and wait expectantly. In that sick-room, with windows open on the little garden and the dusty plain beyond, in that space of quiet and silence suddenly opened amidst loud and labour-filled days—I knew that One was present with us, and took off my shoes.

All clamour of problems ceased; high cadences fell on the inner ear; among the deepening shadows immortal Truth gleamed out, as a human spirit, triumphing over great bodily suffering and the fear of approaching death fared forth into the dark with all its banners of faith and hope flying high.

Was it a Voice? a Silence? an ineffable Communion? a sound of distant music? Who, or what, filled and transfigured the poor room where a humble Indian teacher lay dying?

> "God Almighty, and with Him
> Cherubim and Seraphim,
> Filling all eternity
> Adonai, Elohim."[1]

[1] G. K. Chesterton, *The Holy of Holies*.

CHAPTER XX

TWO BRIDES AND A WIFE

ERANA's daughter was one of the brides. He had been a waif, brought up by kindly Hindu shepherd people. When a stripling, he became a Christian; so his Hindu protectors cast him off. The catechist brought him to the Mission folk, asking if he could be given employment. He seemed very timid, but at home with cattle, so he was put to look after the cow. Gradually he learned the domestic ways of the house and rose from carrying water and washing dishes to putting up tents; then to cooking and waiting at table. He became my general factotum in camp; never very brainy or competent all round, but willing and faithful always. He had a deeply affectionate nature; a good home should have helped him much. Alas, it was denied him. He had turned for marriage arrangements to friends in his old town; they fixed on a pretty, but shiftless and shallow-hearted, girl. There never seemed anything to lay hold of in her character, her ways were ruled by indolence and self-indulgence. She developed a sharp tongue, but no other competence. For years the marriage was childless; at last a little daughter arrived, a great joy to her father's heart. But even her advent could not bring order and discipline into the home. Erana was not one of the strong-minded ones of the earth and did not know how to rule. As Kamala grew up her education was neglected.

"Why is Kamala not at school, Erana?" I inquired many a day, noting his daughter's irregularity.

"My wife likes her to help at home," he defended himself. Lazy Eliza would. And the battle it would have entailed to insist on the child's daily attendance was beyond her father. Direct admonition to Eliza bore fruit for a few days; Kamala turned up at school, but soon stayed away again. She was a dull girl, not keen on the exertions school expected of her. So the years passed, Kamala never got beyond the second standard, though now a lanky, fast-growing girl. Then Erana fell ill. Eliza's nursing could not be relied on, he was taken to the hospital. There had not been much hope from the first; life had dealt hardly by him, and he was tired. For some days he lay, apparently unconscious. The appeal on my part, "Erana, do you know me?" evoked no sign of recognition. But whenever Kamala came and called to him a feeble response of some sort never failed; a faint movement of head or hand, or only a flutter of the lids, betokened the awareness of the father heart. She must have been a burden on his mind to the last.

So he passed to his rest, and lamentation was made over him as a good man who would be held by us all in affectionate remembrance. My thoughts tried to follow him to his new environment. Would he now, I wondered, watch and guard his daughter? For who dare assert that love does not survive; or that, surviving, it is powerless?

The child certainly stood in dire need of help. Eliza took more and more to downward courses. Scandals were rife about her. She had taken in a lodger, a man known to be a rotter; the situation could only be interpreted in one way; but she seemed dead to all shame. She still had a glimmering that her daughter should be kept out of harm's way; for she came to me with a petition to take Kamala into the Home. The pastor came with the same urgent request. Other members of our church came, bombarding me with reasons of which I was already only too conscious. But my quandary was the existence of right and reasonable rules governing the conduct of the Home. Only the children of parents of good repute are admitted. Poor Kamala's living parent did not fulfil that condition. Further, the Boarding Home is not intended to replace Christian parenthood. Where education is available for girls—and the day school is open to any Andapur pupil—they are not eligible for admission. This has at various times meant a battle; responsibility is only too willingly shifted. Our people as yet understand little about the duty of a home, its enormous possibilities and advantages. They see order, happiness, discipline, in the Boarding Home, and calmly sit down to the belief that ordinary homes cannot produce anything like as good —so will the Mission kindly take charge? Apparently, in this world, it is impossible to do good without doing harm at the same time. For this conception of theirs is a definite harm; and, at any rate negatively, one tries to help on the growth of Christian parenthood by this refusal to take Andapur girls. (It has to be remembered that we live in rural parts, and that many of our people are newly come from lower strata of Indian society.) A further reason for this rule is the limitation of our numbers on financial considerations; a girl in headquarters let in might mean a village girl with no chance of further education kept out. There are other rules, about age; a village child must have passed the second standard in the little village school by a certain age. Kamala was long past that.

"It would be putting a premium on parental negligence, for the Mission to step in and try to make good what the parents lost all these years by culpable neglect," I protested to the pastor.

"For her father's sake I will do my best for Kamala," I said to Eliza. "The Home is not open to her—such and such are the rules—but I will get her into a good family. Will you agree to this?"

She did. Arrangements were made with the head master at Ramidi and his wife, outstandingly trustworthy people. But when they arrived to take Kamala with them, Eliza turned round and refused to let her go. The Boarding Home, or nothing.

The bombardment began afresh for me. "Think how

faithfully Erana served you; you must care for the daughter."

To uphold the majesty of law was evidently not my rôle in life. I could not convince our people of it (possibly because I could not convince myself!), they only saw a dire human need. If only Mission work were just the organizations and categories beloved of committees! Unfortunately, it is *people*. And they so often obstinately refuse to fit into categories.

Kamala got into the Home (and I into disgrace with Committee, though they allowed her to stay in the end). She was not a satisfactory pupil in the school, remaining stupid and backward. Nor was she one of the shining lights in the Home; though once or twice, at the weekly drama, I was surprised by flashes of energy and understanding on her part. Was this dull and neglected girl taking in more than appeared to the casual eye?

Eliza's state did not improve. That lodger, indeed, had gone to another town, but there were still uglier rumours now, of her making her home into a loose house; though no one had positive evidence. Kamala had nowhere else to go during the holidays. With an anxious heart I left for for the hills, after a warning talk with the girl. "Your father was a good man; he hoped you would be good."

Then a letter reached me to say that a marriage had been arranged for Kamala by her mother. No details were given. Well, I thought, perhaps that was the best way out of a situation fraught with danger. That is, if the bridegroom were a trustworthy man.

He was not. No one let me know. Perhaps they were all horror-struck; perhaps they felt it was useless, as Eliza was the sole legal guardian, and no one had power to upset her arrangements; possibly they opined that any marriage was better than none, and that as I was due to return in a short time—though after the day fixed—it was soon enough to let me hear bad news.

The bridegroom to be was Eliza's previous lodger and paramour.

No doubt he had noted the growing girl, fresh and youthful beside the faded mother, and had offered Eliza much money, provision for herself, as well as lavish presents for her daughter. So she had concluded the shameful bargain. Everything had apparently been done in great haste; probably Eliza wanted it all to be irrevocable before my return.

She made great preparations; the whole congregation was invited to the wedding feast. They thought of the bride's father and did not like to refuse. The day fixed for the ceremony approached.

Meanwhile what were Kamala's thoughts? That she hated the idea of this marriage is certain; that she understood its peculiarly disgraceful character is probable. She must have been bitterly lonely. Her father had ever been an inarticulate man. Kamala had inherited the same quality. I could not learn that she consulted anyone in her trouble. Perhaps at first she appealed to her mother; if so it was in vain; preparations went forward. She was no match against her mother's temper and tongue. From whence would her help come? Did she in secret appeal to her father, ever remembered as kind and taking her part? Or even higher appeals? Outwardly she kept silence.

The wedding-day dawned. The church was decorated; in due course the band marched up playing; the wedding guests arrived, the bridegroom stood waiting; the pastor was ready to come across to the church from his house in the same compound. Then a distracted Eliza appeared and announced wildly that Kamala could not be found. She had slipped out in the morning, no one knew where; Eliza had thought it was just to a neighbour's house; but when it became time to dress, the bride had not returned; nor was she with neighbours, or in any house in the adjoining Police Lines. The invited guests dispersed to look for the vanished girl. The pastor came over and asked why he was not called, as it was past the appointed time. He, too, joined the search-party.

The band stopped playing and waited for an hour or two, then went home. During the whole afternoon they continued to look for her; in every Christian family and those of old school-fellows; in the old town and in the new town; inquiring everywhere whether anyone had seen her that day. No one had. Fearfully they examined the well in the church compound—to everyone's infinite relief it held no horrible secret. Eliza was weeping, the bridegroom angry; evening came, by then parties were scouring all the country round. The bridegroom demanded back his money and all the jewels; he and Eliza quarrelled violently; he went off by the evening train in a great rage, carrying off the wedding *sari* and jewels, and declaring Eliza had hidden the girl. But the unhappy mother was almost mad; did repentance tear her, as well as anxiety? She must have been aware of the child's utter unwillingness. There were other wells, besides the one in the church compound.

Then, suddenly, in the dark, when everyone concerned had given up the search in despair, Kamala stood amongst them.

"Where have you been?" they all cried out, hardly believing they saw her in the flesh.

"I hid in the vestry," she said calmly. "I did not want this marriage."

"But we looked in there!" they cried.

"Only through the window," said Kamala.

The amazing child had found her own quite simple way out. When no one was by she had slipped into the little room behind the church, not much used by anyone as the pastor had his own house in the compound; she had turned the key and squeezed herself flat against the wall along the floor, directly under the closed window; some boxes in the room she had dragged against her on the other side. In this little narrow space she had lain *perdu.* To searchers looking through the window the room would appear empty; so no one had bothered about the door being locked, thinking the pastor had the key. All day she remained there, without any food, cramped doubtless, hearing the guests arrive in the adjoining church and the band playing, the inquiries and the search going on, and heroically held on to her resolve not to come forth until she heard the night train pass and knew the man would have left. Eliza was so angry with her that she would not have her in the house. The pastor took her in.

Who would have dreamt of such pluck and independence in an Indian girl to whom family pressure and fixed arrangements are traditionally sacred? And Kamala, deemed so dull of wit and void of grit, a descendant from the depressed classes! Here, in desperate need, she had shown astonishing courage and resourcefulness. Perhaps, who can tell, invisible helpers, brought by her father's love, were keeping guard about her throughout that day? And perhaps they, also, had been among the forces pressing me to take her into the Home, and had helped her, while there, to absorb that which would fortify her against her day of need. "*Seeing we also are compassed about with so great a cloud of witnesses . . .*"

The situation still remained precarious. Fortunately many a missionary's study is a match-making bureau. Correspondence with other missions went on briskly and a decent Christian man became Kamala's husband; Eliza, that rudderless ship—tired, maybe, of the mockery and ridicule pointed at her—giving her consent.

* * * * *

Other matrimonial troubles came my way.

"People waiting to see you," announced Rama Sami one fine morning while I was at *chota hazri.*

A young couple stood in the verandah. Their clothes were good, but worn and soiled as from travel; the girl wore jewels, and smiled happily and confidently. But the youth looked at me with a shade of anxiety.

"Please help us to get married," he said.

I rubbed my eyes. Had I waked up in a Western country to-day? In India, with its immemorial marriage customs among all its races and throughout all strata of its society, this request was amazing.

"Have you no people?" I asked.

They had plenty, it appeared, both of them; but cast out by all. By degrees they told their story.

The lad was a member of a Christian community come over from the Lingaits, a sect in South India founded originally in the revolt against caste, but now merely an additional one and as strict as any in most ways. The girl belonged to it. The Christian community had excommunicated the boy for becoming involved with a Hindu girl and holding on to her; the young woman's people were trying to force her into a Lingait marriage. Adventurously and gaily they had broken loose from their old moorings and run away together.

So here, unexpectedly, I was confronted by romance.

"We lived in neighbouring houses in our village," they explained. What did differences in sect and caste and religion matter when youth met youth?

One could picture the sunny village; the adjoining houses and perhaps gardens; the children playing together and growing up together; when the boy's parents became Christians it meant probably little to him. The girl's people seemed to have left her marriage till rather late; the original Lingaits revolted against child-marriage among other caste tyrannies, and there is still more freedom among them than among orthodox Hindus, though that freedom has its distinct limits! as our young people found. Their meetings continued,—stolen, who knows, in their own gardens? village gossip must have arisen; parental interference and threats followed; when they obstinately clung to each other their respective communities stepped in. So they had fled, wandering over the country; received nowhere by either Christians or Lingaits, having gone against the sanctions of each society.

"Please find me a post and help us to get married," the young man reiterated.

Easier said than done. A Christian marriage is a legal as well as a social contract, unlike a Hindu marriage, which is a religious one only (and therefore indissoluble). Christian marriages are only permitted between Christians; parties to any arrangements of marriage between Christians and non-Christians are liable to jail. Then baptize her, and get over the legal difficulty. Without instruction, without repentance, as a mere formality? For however natural the course of true love might be, and however strongly I might be sympathizing with their bold bid for freedom—they were not selfless martyrs or altruistic pioneers on behalf of others; they had each gone against their own conscience and the laws of their community; they were, quite truly, "sinners"; and in their lawless and homeless wanderings had begun to taste the fruit of self-willed ways. No wonder the lad looked at me anxiously.

"I will never marry anyone but her; I only want work and a respectable home for us both," he urged.

They were victims, as well as sinners; victims of rigid social conditions and antagonisms; how beautifully and naturally their relationship might have developed and flowered under ideal laws which allowed for individual cases as well as preserving the general good. How many such frustrations must be happening constantly in India, with its caste tyrannies and limitations!

Perplexedly I looked at them.

"I will help you," I said at last, "if you will do what I say. You must here and now separate and cease your lawless living together. Sivamma will be sent to a Home where she will receive instruction, as soon as it can be arranged. You, Lingappa, must promise not to follow her, nor to come to this compound while she is here. I will try and find work for you."

Separation was a difficult pill to swallow, but they promised everything in the end.

Chits were sent all over the place, and finally work in the Police was obtained for the young man. Meanwhile, until arrangements for her reception could be made, the girl was saddled upon me; her people would not have her back, she could not be left in the street, so the question of her lodgment, food, occupation, instruction, fell to my day's share of perplexing jobs. She could not be put into the Boarding Home, she was not "good." Fortunately, Lois from Ramidi happened to be in for medical treatment; the girl lodged with her and was put to help with watering the garden. She turned out to be obedient, quiet, and industrious. But also she seemed to possess an irresistible attraction for the other sex. There were men-servants about, notes addressed to her were found; anxiety was my portion and watchfulness my hourly task. Most thankful and relieved I was when arrangements for her departure to the Home were at last completed, though there was a battle royal with her young man when it came to her actual leaving. He had kept his promise of not coming to the compound; but the Sunday service offered entrancing chances of a sight of his beloved across the church—how could he forgo that? He was not the first young man in history, I believe, who went to church with this motive.

The story ended happily; the period of discipline was not prolonged unduly; after some months of instruction and good behaviour Sivamma was baptized in the Home. The young police recruit obtained leave to go there and they were married on the spot. Long life and happiness to them!

* * * * *

After these problems among the Christian folk I found another encounter—brief as it was—the more refreshing. In the ladies' hot little waiting-room of the junction twenty miles from Andapur I was doomed to wait some hours for the train on the other line. A young Brahmin girl entered, followed by an older woman carrying a child. The older woman was evidently a servant, and presently went out. The other looked so young and girlish that it was almost a shock to me to see her sit down to nurse the baby. So this charming child, playing with her little son in the most bewitching fashion when his hunger was appeased, had been a mother for two years, and was presently to be a mother again.

"Are you travelling alone?" I asked.

"Yes, with the servant. My husband is transferred to Bellary; he has gone on to find a house for us."

The baby objected to our talking; though I shielded my awful face with my fan nothing would do but a complete blocking-out of the horizon containing that repulsive whiteness. I watched in fascination the ways of the young mother as she laid him on the bench and herself beside him till he was pacified and at last asleep; there was a dignity and a grace about her that roused admiration. While peace reigned we continued making acquaintance.

"My mother-in-law died a year ago; there is no aunt or anyone living with us. It would be awkward to have them, as my husband is in Government service and gets transferred so often; it is difficult to find rooms in new places sometimes. "No," in answer to my question about future arrangements, "no one can come for my confinement. We have so few relations. But I have the servant," she added bravely; and then, proudly pointing to her son, "I had him all by myself too, only the servant with me."

The bravery of her, still a child herself. Bless her for her courage!

The talk with her opened a vista of what official ways may mean at times for young wives; transferred here and there, perhaps to another language area,—loosened from the patriarchal Indian system of families living together; the husband being absent all day in his office, etiquette making it difficult to seek other women's acquaintance; sometimes, as with my little fellow-traveller, having to face unsupported the ordeal of maternity.

Yet how graciously and bravely this daughter of India bore herself towards life and its difficulties. The chance encounter made an indelible impression.

The admiration and sympathy she compelled caused many thoughts, strengthened still more by the recollection of the two recent brides. If Kamala of low-caste origin could suddenly throw off the spirit of servility and fear; if Sivamma in her Lingait village was ready to set forth on adventure of uncertain issue at the behest of human love; if this young high-caste girl without any previous training in independence or enterprise could calmly and courageously face trying and lonely situations: could, without the traditional direction of elder women, adapt herself to, and, in a sense, take command of, new and strange circumstances —then the spirit of the heroic women of Aryan history is not dead. Has the fire smouldered secretly in the hearts of Indian women through the centuries? Has India's womanhood, through the many years of its subjection and endurance, developed qualities of fortitude and courage and self-discipline which will work out the salvation of the whole race?

CONCLUSION

From a little English home and garden I listen for news of the beloved country.

The Sarada Act had been passed by the Indian Legislative Assembly; no longer will there be the martyrdom of child-wives. No? While these pages are being compiled I hear of many deputations waiting upon Governors and other authorities asking for the Act to be repealed. Meanwhile, moneylenders are having the time of their lives in paying out sums to borrowers hastening on the marriage of every daughter they have before the Act comes into legal force; even of infants a few months old who have to be carried to the ceremony. Is, then, public opinion converted to the Act? And if not, what evasions may yet take place?

The Untouchables are now declared to be part of the whole body of Hinduism. Their demand to enter temples is held to be justified. Mahatma Gandhi receives them in his *Ashram*, where they associate with those of high caste; and where high-caste people take their turn at those menial services for the community formerly relegated to out-castes. Will this accomplish the destruction of the shudder of repulsion and disgust felt by the ordinary caste man at the approach of the outcaste? Hardly.

As an indication that it is by no means gone the following may be mentioned.

Many great temples hitherto open to all comers—secure in the assurance that no cursed outcaste would dare to come near—have now closed their doors to all. For permission to enter a pass is required. How simple a preventive against Undesirables—while the theory of equality is upheld. Public feeling is as yet far from being truly changed.

Yet the voices of reformers are growing louder, their numbers stronger—if only they would not commit the disastrous error of confusing politics with religion! What fills me with pride and hope is that women are so increasingly of their number. That, for instance, a woman should be the Vice-President of a Provincial Legislative Council, that she should work so devotedly and strenuously in the cause of child-wives and widows, and of temple girls, is a fact full of significance and promise. But I remember also her saying to me on the one occasion when I had the privilege of meeting her, "A friend of mine is dying of cancer. She is still young; she is rebellious and afraid. I do not know what to say to help her. Is there anything that can be said? I cannot find anything in our Hindu religion."

And there comes other news these days, altogether grievous—of missing the way of trust, of belief that the other side can mean well. Surely the world will never be saved or conquered by anything but faith, faith in the motive of your neighbour, whatever his faults, for one. But to doubt the ultimate issue—through whatever cost of suffering it may have to emerge—were to doubt the ceaseless pressure of the Spirit of God on the spirit of man. Are we not all learning together, however slowly?

"The great knowledge of life," says Dr. Albert Schweitzer, "is to learn how to deal with your disappointments. . . . Life must not rob us of our ideals; we must grow into them." Thinking thereon the words which form the title of this book came to me.

It is not only missionary lives which have to take uphill steps. May one not view a whole country as struggling upwards?

India loves uphill steps. Where rocks rise suddenly from the plain, or wherever the country is at all mountainous, one cannot go far without seeing a gleam of white on a summit, indicating the wall of a temple or a shrine. From the top of the cone-shaped hill near Andapur such a gleam greeted me every morning. Wherever one sees it one knows that rough steps are cut in rock or stone, or built on earthen slopes, leading to the desired goal of worship. On the temple's own special day, many pilgrims will climb painfully that upward path to offer their gifts and their devotion.

May one take it as a parable? In spite of all that now darkens the horizon and utterly clouds the atmosphere, making faith and trust so hard to come by—are there not those gleams of white on distant mountain-tops? Steep and difficult must be the steps leading to those heights. Some, maybe, are not yet hewn. Perhaps it is only the light shining from the Sign on Another Hill which can disperse fogs of mutual distrust, and awaken in us all the spirit of humility and sacrifice without which no redemption can be brought about.

